T0381180

Ask and You Shall **Receive**

Ask and You Shall **Receive**

What did you ask for
when you got up this morning?

Pierre **Morency**

PARTRIDGE
A Penguin Random House Company

Pierre Morency
55-5764 Avenue de Monkland, Montreal, Quebec, Canada H4A 1E9
www.pierremorency.com
question@pierremorency.com

Print information available on the last page.

To order additional copies of this book, contact
Partridge India
000 800 10062 62
orders.india@partridgepublishing.com

www.partridgepublishing.com/india

Contents

Contents

Acknowledgements

This may sound like a bit of a cliché, but please forgive me for refraining from naming everybody who took part in the experiments that led to this book. If I did, I'd probably have a list of 10,000 names generated over the last 21 years. So instead, let me just say thank you to one and all.

I do want to specifically express my heartfelt gratitude to my gurus: my children, Charlie, Timmy, Jaimee, Amy, Jesse; my partner, Jessy (God only knows how patient this woman is); my parents, Gaura das, Nirvana Muni, Francis Hosein, and Satchi—oh! I almost forgot—and Albert Einstein!

Thanks also to my publisher, Jean Paré, who succeeded in keeping my two feet solidly on the surface of the earth (not an easy task) and helped me produce a comprehensible and realistic book. Of course, who is to say in what sphere of reality his realism lies? That, as we will see, is a whole other story!

Finally, thanks in advance to you, dear reader, for having the audacity to embark on this trip.

1

Warming Up

My grandfather was a successful businessman—at first. But after running many flourishing businesses in Quebec City and after a series of nebulous events, he lost just about everything he owned. I was only nine at the time, yet he decided that my life should be devoted to learning the laws of success all the better to understand what happened to him and how he got knocked flat on his back. My education began on a Sunday afternoon with selected readings from *The Power of Your Subconscious Mind* by Joseph Murphy.

'Everything you obtain in life', he read, 'comes from your subconscious mind. The subconscious is the true interpreter of your deepest thoughts.'

You're right, of course. The effect of words like these on a child of that age is obviously transient. Still, the seed was sown in my mind. My entire life since then has centred around one great passion: the search for the secrets of success.

A scientist by training, I never cease to marvel at how little I actually know about this extraordinary universe in which we live. I am also saddened to observe how few people actually take the trouble to try to incorporate the laws of nature into their mental and intellectual lives. Most of us are simply content to live lives of stunted highs and lows, picayune dreams, and minor disappointments.

I am a physicist, and by nature, I am interested in tasting all that life has to offer. If I have learned one vital thing from my experiments, it is this: the flavour of life changes tremendously according to the way you live it.

Oh, but I can already hear you saying to yourself, 'Where is this guy coming from? He's a physicist, for heaven's sake, a scientist, and yet he spends his time studying success, happiness, and wealth.' (I forgot to add that I am also a marketing freak; I even wrote a bestselling book on the subject in 2001.) And yes, I get asked this question almost every day!

My answer is astonishingly simple. Physics is a science by which we try to explain natural phenomena using somewhat eccentric hypotheses, imagining experiments to test our theories and analyzing facts. Well, it is just as feasible to analyze success, marketing, wealth, and happiness using similar techniques, and in this book, I'm going to show you how.

Are you seeking a different life, looking for the means by which you can attain your goals and make your dreams come true? This book will help you understand that if you really want to change your life, you first need to have the audacity to just ask.

That is my humble advice to you. Ask, ask, and never stop asking. The more you ask, the more you'll get.

So let's start. Go get a pencil and a sheet of paper. Come on, come on, right away. All right. Now, write down three questions you want to resolve that prompted you to buy this book or three situations you want to change in your life with the help of this book. Write them down. Don't just keep them in your head. The more precise your questions are, the more precise your answers will be. Go on now, write!

But whatever you do, don't write down that you were simply curious. That's not going to get you anywhere. And don't write down that you bought the book because somebody told you about a character named Pierre Morency who walks around in his stockinged feet all the time and has been conducting scientific experiments on success for twenty years and has compiled a summary of his results in a book entitled *Ask and You Shall Receive*.

If curiosity is your only reason for reading this, you're missing the point. Simple curiosity will not lead you to the most important lesson to be learned from this book: the secret of the discoveries that I have made over the years in my business meetings all across Canada and the United States and even in the hidden grottoes of mysterious India.

But for now, let's forget about understanding the why. Let's handle the how first. So again, simply write down three questions that you have about your life, your success, your wealth, your relationships, whatever—anything you like.

'Ask and you shall receive.' Everybody knows that quote from the Bible, right? So what did you ask for when you got up this morning? Nothing, right? Well, if you asked for nothing when you awoke, that's just what you will have received by the time you're ready to go to sleep tonight: nothing at all!

It's a powerful but simple rule. If you ask for nothing precise, you'll get precisely nothing. One of the main objectives of this book is to teach you exactly how to develop the reflex of always asking for something from life and how to always make each new request bigger than the last.

So if your page is still blank, get that pencil going. Three questions—let's just begin with that. You'll be astonished at the power of a sentence as simple as 'Ask and you shall receive'. But if everything is perfect in your life, if you have nothing to ask for, well then, this book will be of no use to you. Give it to a friend or put it away until you realize that there is something you want to ask for.

The truth of the matter is that you will get answers as big, or as small, as your questions. It's that straightforward. So go ahead, for Pete's sake, ask for a lot, a whole lot!

What's So Great about Success Anyway?

Success isn't everything; there's more to life than just that, isn't there? I hear some of you saying that. Everyone talks the talk, but do we really have to spend all our waking (and dreaming) hours running after success? Is it all that important? And anyway, what do we really mean by success?

Good questions, all of them, and a good place to start.

At 6 a.m., wakey-wakey!

Three hits on the snooze button, then a little voice in your ear whispers that you'd better get up if you want to have time to shower, breakfast, and take out the garbage.

The kids are dressed—finally—and you're now up to cruising speed, jumping into the car, on the road, slamming on the brakes to avoid crashing into the jerk who has just cut you off, and simultaneously doing the sitting Watusi to avoid the coffee splashing out of the holder and on to your business suit.

With the kids parked safely at school, it's office time. You smile quick hellos to your colleagues, flick on the computer, and summarily scan the 47 (or is it 470?) overnight emails, most of them get-rich-quick pyramid schemes, enlarge-your-private-parts propositions, and endless photos of all creatures great and small in endless sexual positions that come to you because once—once!—out of naive curiosity, you visited a Web porn site.

You look at your watch, your Daytimer, and your to-do list. A mild grumbling from your stomach gets you mulling over the time left until lunch. The cranberry muffin wolfed down in the car with the dregs of the coffee was obviously not enough to carry you through the morning. (Note to yourself for tomorrow: make it a double.)

When after an hour's scrupulous reading of every section in the daily you finally get to your horoscope, you discover that today is propitious for falling in love. How about that? A little spice in your life! After a quick detour to the washroom for a mirror check (your look is satisfactory), it's time to start working.

It's just 10 a.m.

Lunchtime is bank time—well, ATM time anyway. You check once more that there is enough in your account for the monthly car payment and pick up a pack of cigarettes at the convenience store. Amazing, the price has gone up again. The government bureaucrats obviously get the fact that squeezing out of you a few more pennies for the tax revenue won't lessen your need to light up as you finish your sandwich outside the door to your office building.

In the afternoon, though half asleep, you half-heartedly continue your work, daydreaming about the movie you'll want to rent on Friday night, a movie you'll watch in your comfortable recliner while knocking back a couple of brewskies as you celebrate the weekend that has arrived oh too slowly.

At 5 p.m. (finally!) you're homeward-bound, docked, deplaned, and through the airlock. You just have time to turn on the tube and catch the headlines for the fifth time today.

Supper is thrown together and quickly gulped down the hatch so you have ten minutes to play a little Nintendo and set your youngest to homework. Now at last, you can plonk yourself down in front of the TV for the evening's entertainment: travel, adventure, romance, and action, enough to keep your mind wandering until bedtime. In fact, as you watch, you think about all the people who are suffering in other countries, and you mutter to yourself as you climb the stairs to your bedroom that your life isn't so bad after all. You fall asleep on this thought. Then the 6 a.m. alarm sounds, and the whole circus starts all over again.

Terrific, isn't it? What a life! The acme of excitement, really. You've got an enviable life that is truly worth living. If your life fits any part of this scenario, maybe it's time to ask yourself again why you should have any interest in success. Oh, yeah!

Vacation and the island paradise on earth

Perhaps you have never given it much thought, but in fact, you are really lucky to be alive. Think about it. What if you were never born? 'I don't exist.' Gives you a strange feeling, doesn't it?

But you do exist. You're really here. Not only are you alive, but if you think about it, you have very few important responsibilities. Oh, sure, you have tasks, lots of tasks. But how many of your activities are really necessary? Truthfully, very few.

As long as we're at it, if you're asking yourself why you are here on this earth, I have an answer for you, one that should give you some peace of mind. Believe it or not, you are here on vacation.

In fact, your purpose in life is to consciously live out all your wildest dreams right to the day when you think you have tasted everything you can possibly taste in your human form. And what a privilege it is to have been issued this kind of suit, but don't worry, you deserve it. You deserve this life, so you ought to take advantage of it. Live it to the max.

Still have doubts about your fabulous luck so far? Read on!

You are the chosen one

Take out your calculator. Come on, I'm waiting.

Let's do it by the numbers. There are more than 400 million sperm cells in every male ejaculation. Now, supposing that your father is the most chaste of men, he probably only had at least 10 ejaculations in his life. And your mother, like most women, has had between 400 and 500 ovulations in the course of her childbearing years.

So 400 million multiplied by at least 10 gives us 4 billion; multiply that by 500 eggs, and it's equal to 2 trillion possible combinations—and if your father was anywhere near sexually normal, an awful lot more! In other words, the probability of your existence was less than one in two trillion at best. And yet, here you are! So relax. You're it, the winner of the biggest lottery in the universe. You are the 'chosen' sperm!

All right, calm down now

Welcome to paradise on earth.

Believe it or not, you and I both live in an earthly paradise—on vacation. That's why they call it paradise on earth!

You held the winning ticket and won a trip to the best Club Med in the universe for the tiniest fraction of universal time—60 to 100 years. Hardly an instant, if you think about the billions of years the universe has been around.

In fact, the most recent astronomical calculations estimate that at least 14 billion years have elapsed since the Big Bang, the initial explosion that gave birth to our universe. Compared to that, what is a span of a hundred years? Nothing at all. A window of consciousness hardly an iota wide. So it's about time you take advantage of this vacation you're on, don't you think?

'Sure, some vacation. You spend your youth studying, then you have to struggle to find a job. Once you have one, you lose the best years of your life working like a dog to pay the mortgage and support your spouse and kids and take a couple of weeks' vacation. Then you have to put aside money for your—hopefully—ten years of well-earned retirement, during which most of your savings will be spent on the medicine you need to stay alive and healthy. Some vacation. Had I known this was the trip, I would have fired my travel agent and found a new one!'

I understand what you're saying. But it's only one point of view. And it's one I personally don't share. There is really no good reason to look at life this way just because most people do. Remember, on this island paradise of ours, everything is possible. It's your choice. You can be out enjoying a walk on the beach, or you can stay locked in your room with the curtains drawn tight, muttering about the lack of sunshine in your life.

The truth is, the most beautiful rose garden is also full of thorns. And if you spent all your time complaining about the thorns, well, you won't have much time to enjoy the roses.

The macho effect

'Stop dreaming!'

'Pierre, have you lost your mind?'

'Pierre, what you're saying makes no sense!'

Hold on just a minute there. I know what you're thinking, and I've heard it all before—a lot.

'You have to work hard to get ahead.'

'You can't have everything in life.'

'You have to plan ahead.'

'You have to protect yourself.'

'You have to provide for your children's education.'

'You have to put aside money for when you grow old.'

'You have to . . .'

Yadda yadda yadda.

If you repeat this mantra often enough, of course, you will end up believing it. Worse, you will end up being proud of it, you know, as in:

'Bob, last week I put in almost ninety hours. Practically slept at my desk.'

'Wow, Monica, that's impressive. You're really getting ahead.'

Do you think that boasting to your parents, friends, and colleagues about how hard you work really gets you anywhere? It only gets you closer to the peace you'll find when this trip is over.

So as they say in Westerns, 'Stick 'em up. Your job or your life!'

Okay. Let me apologize now for being so in your face right from the start, but I haven't got time everlasting to shake you out of your torpor and your well-oiled system of beliefs. We're already well into the book, and if I want to help you change and share some of my research on this subject, the gloves have to come off. So answer me this: would you trade your life for your job? Put like that, of course not. Nobody would.

But that's exactly what you are doing! Think about it. Your entire life is built around preparing to get a job, getting a job, servicing that job, and keeping the job. It's so true that most of us are at our wit's end after the first day's vacation. You don't think so? Well, take this challenge. Next weekend or next time you have two days off, try no TV, no newspapers, and no activities at all that are the least bit work related.

If you can get through a weekend like that without climbing the walls out of boredom, then maybe you're ready for the rest of this book.

Thinking time

Do you know what distinguishes humans from horses, cows, and pigs? After all, we eat, sleep, copulate, and work, just like the animals. What we humans are capable of is thought!

And how much of your week is spent thinking? How many hours of your busy schedule, when you're walking around scratching your head and wondering how to make yourself more efficient and your life more intense, are set aside exclusively for just that?

Do you see what I'm getting at?

If you don't take the time to think about how to improve your efficiency on the job and the tone of your life in general, who do you think will?

In your place of work, who spends time thinking? At home, how much time is spent just thinking about life? If the answers to these questions are nobody and none, are you any better than the cows, horses, and pigs?

> You have to limit your work week to thirty hours at most and take at least one full day off each week to spend simply thinking. This thinking day must not be spent at your place of work.

'Pierre, that's ridiculous! I already can't keep up. I can't take time off just to think!'

Not true. You are always short on time precisely because you never take time off to consider how you could accomplish the same work in less time. And don't give me the line about having a strict employer, a rigid job contract, being paid by the hour, and so forth and so on.

Do you really think that people who have the best lives put in 90 hours a week? Come on! Do you think that people who earn 10 times or 100 times your salary work 10 times or 100 times more than you?

Of course not!

People who succeed in life are the ones who work the least. Fewer hours on the job equals more wealth.

But these people take the time to put together a system of methods to maximize their efficiency and to give themselves the possibility of living a more exciting life than the average Joe. That's all.

The story of a very special employee

'My boss never wants to listen to the suggestions I make. Why should I spend any time looking for new ideas?'

Does this sound familiar?

I met a lady who worked in customer service at an American bank. Her annual salary was $22,500. She told me that one day she came up with a terrific idea that would increase the bank's profitability. Since she met many of the branch's clients during the course of her day, she was in fact well placed to gauge their needs and the challenges facing her company.

She took a few moments to present her idea to a superior, who rejected it out of hand without even taking the time to analyze the details of what she had come up with.

I asked her this question: 'Are you convinced that your idea would be efficient and profitable for the bank?'

She thought it through and replied, 'I'd walk on nails for it. My idea would only cost $10,000 to implement and would bring back at least $40,000 in less than thirty days. That's a 400 per cent return in only one month!'

I replied, 'All right, you'd walk on nails for it, but would you bet your salary on it?'

She thought about it overnight, and the following day, she told me that in fact her work was kind of monotonous and she would have no trouble finding another job at that salary. So here is what she did.

She asked her branch manager to let her implement the project at her own expense. If her idea failed to bring in the rewards she estimated, she would pay for all the costs involved out of her own salary. But if her innovation was successful, she wanted one-third of the profit it brought in for two full years.

Her audacity paid off. The bank accepted her proposal, and not only did she double her salary, she was promoted twice in the following year.

2

The Scientific Principles of Success

Just Go Ahead and Ask, for Heaven's Sake!

I'm just a plain old physicist. I'm not here to tell you how to live or why you've been put on this earth. I am just interested in sharing the fruits of my research and my observations with you. Why am I writing all this down? To empty my mind and make space for new experiences. As for you, you can do what you like with the information. That's your problem, not mine.

But I can tell you one thing for sure: I have never met a single person who was not living exactly the life he or she asked for every day.

> You are living the exact life you ask for.

The universe works mathematically. Whether you look at the precision of the movement of the planets, the impeccable regularity of the seasons, or the marvellous symbiosis between living beings, everything is predictable.

You are living the life you ask for simply because it can happen in no other way. Your existence is the precise mirror of your daily thoughts.

What, you want a more 'scientific' explanation? You'll just have to get your mind around the incontestable fact that your thoughts create your life.

You've certainly heard this before, but today even the most sceptical of physicists are forced to conclude from their own experiments that matter is nothing more than pure energy and energy is nothing more, and nothing less, than consciousness!

If a thought is generated by consciousness, which generates energy, which in turn then becomes matter, it is easy to see that your thoughts create matter through a completely scientific process!

So if you want to change your life, my friend, the solution is simple. Change your thoughts first!

I could end this book here. After all, I just put the whole book into one sentence. Everything that the greatest human minds ever came up with—whether it's Jesus, Buddha, Mohammed, Einstein, or Heisenberg—really amounts to the same message: ask and you shall receive.

But what about how you will receive? Ah, but that's not our business, neither yours nor mine. We are not sufficiently intelligent to figure that one out. It doesn't matter anyway. Look, there may be billions of variables that go into answering that part of the question. We humans have trouble enough managing two or three variables at a time. But billions? Fugeddahboudit! We're not built for the how but for the why and the what.

When you're dining at a five-star restaurant, you don't waste time wondering how the chef came up with the attractive and tasty food on your plate. You order, you eat, you enjoy. Full stop. There is nothing more to say, really, unless you want to take the roundabout way and justify absolutely everything.

Oh, yes, I know, you don't find this intellectually satisfying. Too facile. You haven't made enough of an effort to be able to succeed right away. You want to deserve it when you enter paradise. You want to have earned it by the sweat of your brow.

Fine. You want details? Here they come. But remember, I'm doing this just because you want to complicate your life. And it could have been so simple!

Kissimmee cats

Last summer, I went to Florida for a few weeks with my wife and three kids. We camped in Kissimmee, right near the gates of Walt Disney World. One evening, we were looking up at the full moon when a group of cats appeared out of nowhere. There were all sorts of them: a big black cat that seemed to be the leader, a mother with two little kittens, a cream-tailed one that was making a ruckus, and a large tom that looked like a panther and seemed shunned by the others.

I brought out a bowl of milk, some bread, and a plate of gourmet spaghetti and watched them eat, admiring the spontaneity of their lives. What would they have eaten, I wondered, had we not been in their path or had they happened on less neighbourly campers?

In fact, it was a good lesson for me. These wild cats took their next meal for granted, and so quite naturally, they somehow got it.

Getting all worked up about our future only makes it more distant and more difficult to obtain.

A pound of butter

The wild cats episode brings to mind a quote from the Bible in reference to birds. 'Even they neither sow nor reap, yet the Heavenly Father doth feed them.'

The fears we nourish about not having enough money, food, clothing, or means in life literally give birth to these very problems.

Whatever your circumstances, you likely have butter in the fridge. Well, is butter easier to obtain than wealth, a house, or a luxury car? No, not easier, just different in scale, just different in the scale of your thoughts.

I know you believe that it is harder to make $100,000 a year than it is to make $30,000. That's where your problem lies. As long as, in your mind, money is harder to obtain than butter, it will remain harder to obtain in your life.

> I can guarantee you that $1,000,000,000 is no more difficult to earn than $10,000. Not more difficult, just different.

Look, do you think it is more difficult to fly from Montreal to London than from Montreal to Boston? Of course not. It is obviously not more difficult, just longer, you think.

Really? What if you bicycled to Boston, while I took the Concorde to London? Which trip would take the most time?

A ham story

When I was a young man, my mother would prepare baked ham for dinner on occasion. Whenever she served the meat, it was sliced from both ends, and I always found that odd. One day I let my curiosity get the better of me and asked why she served the ham this way. Why not just start slicing from one end? Somewhat surprised at my question, my mom replied, 'That's the way your grandma taught me.'

I immediately grabbed the telephone and dialled my grandmother's number.

'Grandma, why do you always slice ham from both ends before you serve it?'

'Why, child, that's just the way your great-grandmother did it. That's the way I learned it from her.'

Alas, I was unable to reach my great-grandmother by phone in the hereafter. But I was able to discover with some prodding of memories that my great-grandmother had a very small oven. The ham she got from the butcher wouldn't fit, so she sliced off a little at each end to be able to cook it.

Three generations later, the ham was being nipped off at the ends for no reason at all except tradition!

It was a good life lesson. Most of our beliefs and habits, both yours and mine, arose from necessity and are no more immutable than my mom's sliced baked ham.

Aristotle and Galileo

You want another example? Okay, here is another 'ham story'. Hold on to your hat; you're going to find this one incredible.

The first player in the piece is: Aristotle, a Greek philosopher, disciple of Plato, and hero of the fourth century BC. He became famous for his astounding ability to reason. He would cram logic into students' heads for generations. He believed that metaphysics was the foundation of physics, which had a natural tendency to evolve towards perfection.

Next is Galileo (1564–1642), a mathematician, philosopher, and physicist. At the age of nineteen, he discovered the laws governing the movement of the pendulum while he was observing a chandelier in the cathedral at Pisa.

In the left corner, ladies and gentlemen, is Aristotle, the logical brain, and, in the right, Galileo, the scientific experimenter. The challenge: to find the correct theory of how objects fall to earth.

Aristotle claimed that if we drop two different objects simultaneously, one twice as heavy as the other, the heavier one will, out of necessity, fall twice as fast as the lighter one.

But is this true? You can easily find out for yourself. Holding a light object in your right hand and an object at least twice as heavy in your left, climb up on a chair and let both objects drop at the same time.

Well? Was Aristotle right? Did the heavier object hit the ground in half the time it took for the lighter object as the celebrated master of logic predicted? No. The objects hit the ground simultaneously.

So what's my point? Simply this: Galileo invented a basic experiment that would demonstrate the correctness or error in Aristotle's logic. He climbed to the top of the Tower of Pisa with cannonballs of various weights (some claim this is when the Tower began to lean!) and dropped them. To the astonishment of the scientific world at that time, all the cannonballs hit the earth simultaneously.

It took 1,800 years to disprove through simple experimentation the false beliefs that had been taught, learned, and passed down through the generations simply because everyone relied on taught logic instead of testing Aristotle's theory.

One more 'ham story'.

Programming your beliefs

Your life is the fruit of your thoughts as we already said. But where do these thoughts originate? Where are their roots?

If you think of the brain as a powerful computer, your thoughts would be like the messages you read on the terminal screen. These messages come from the programming in the software being used. It's the same for you and all your life experiences. Everything depends on the software of your beliefs.

Let's take a sample of your beliefs to see what your 'on-board computer' has to work with. Keep in mind that each of your beliefs is a trigger for the experiences of your life.

- You believe that money doesn't bring you happiness.
- You believe you shouldn't put all your eggs in the same basket.
- You believe you have to have a safety hatch.
- You believe you have to protect yourself with insurance policies, patents, an alarm system, and a pension fund.
- You believe you need to put money aside for your retirement. And there are more . . .
- You believe that sinning will take you to the gates of hell and good behaviour will get you to heaven.
- You believe that you have to eat meat to absorb the protein your muscles require.
- You believe you have to exercise to lose weight.
- You believe that the more you smoke, the more you risk getting cancer.
- You believe that ejaculation (both male and female) is synonymous with orgasm.
- You believe that parents have a responsibility to educate their children.
- You believe that you can actually help others in life.

The last one is my personal favourite. I really like this particular belief.

It's the hit parade of your beliefs in your asset column. And we're only scratching the surface.

I'm not pointing fingers here, by the way. Think about it: every time you point one finger at someone, you're also pointing three fingers at yourself. Go ahead, try it. It's something to consider. I'm only trying to show you to what degree your life is governed by a whole series of completely destructive beliefs that have no more reason for existing than the 'ham story' I brought up a few pages ago.

Take a moment to analyze the consequences of these beliefs on your life. Be critical of yourself; observe your life truthfully. Now, let's take another look at the beliefs we listed earlier.

• Money doesn't bring you happiness.

It doesn't surprise me that you don't have much or enough money in your life. If you program the computer to seek happiness and, at the same time, tell it that money doesn't bring happiness, how do you think the computer will behave when faced with opportunities to make money?

• You shouldn't put all your eggs in the same basket.

If you take the trouble to open your eyes, forget what you read in the newspapers, and look objectively at the lives of those people who are most successful and who have the most pleasure in life, you will quickly realize that, on the contrary, they do put all their eggs in the same basket. Sure, they break the occasional egg or two, but who cares? They put more eggs in the basket, that's all. Remember, you can't make an omelette without breaking an egg!

• You have to have a safety hatch.

To discover new continents, you have to be ready to lose sight of your accustomed shores. As long as you feel the need for a safety hatch, you'll never throw yourself completely into a new project. Your brain will always interpret the safety hatch as a possibility of failure and put into motion the means to fail.

• You have to protect yourself with insurance policies, patents, an alarm system, and a pension fund.

Protect yourself against what? The only thing you really need protection from is suffocation from your own beliefs. And I have yet to see an insurance policy sold for that risk!

• You need to put money aside for your retirement.

That's right. You spend your whole active life working yourself to death, ruining your health so you can use your retirement savings to pay for medicine and doctors' bills. Now there's a winning formula!

• Sinning will take you to the gates of hell, and good behaviour will get you to heaven.

I love studying religions. I'm not talking about the human organizations that built religious movements, but the sacred texts and great masters who heeded their own teachings in their lives. All of them tell us that paradise is in the present moment. They also teach that God is omnipresent. If God is everywhere, he is here. How could God be anything but wonderful?

• You have to eat meat to absorb the protein your muscles require.

The goal of this book is not to offer a short course on gastronomy or to promote vegetarianism. Still, it is crystal clear that your body and your consciousness (remember that matter becomes energy, which turns into consciousness) run at the frequency of what you eat and absorb.

Try this simple experiment: For seven consecutive days, eat only one kind of meat. Keep a diary of your emotions, your sexual appetite, the restfulness or agitation of your sleep—in other words, your body's and your brain's reactions to your diet and the kind of thoughts going through your mind. The following week, eat neither meat nor eggs and make the same observations.

You will definitely notice a difference in the way your body runs. It's a completely physical phenomenon. Still, I'm happy in a carnivorous world. Keeps the others from eating all the food we vegetarians enjoy.

• You have to exercise to lose weight.

I'm not here to tell you to avoid all physical activity—on the contrary. But you should know that there are countless people in this world who hardly exercise at all and yet have no trouble controlling their weights. Still, before attributing this to genetics and heredity (another belief here as genes are themselves just 'materialized' thoughts), let's take a closer look at your beliefs about weight and diets.

For example, you think that by reducing your intake of fat, you will automatically lose weight. You also think that animal protein is more important and more potent than vegetable protein. Well, the fact of the matter is that there are so many old wives' tales in the field of nutrition that the 'food beliefs software' of the average individual can easily crash.

The Italians drink more wine than the British and have a lower rate of heart attacks. But the Chinese drink even less than the Brits and yet they too have a lower rate of heart problems. The French have more fat in their diet, and yet they also have fewer heart problems. But the Japanese eat less fat than the British, and guess what, they too enjoy a lower rate of heart disease.

What does this all mean? Eat and drink all you want, but don't be born British? All kidding aside, for each dietary regime, there will always be someone to offer its opposite and offer cases of success. The important common point here: beliefs.

• The more you smoke, the more you risk getting cancer.

If you believe that the more you smoke, the greater your chances are of getting lung cancer, you must not smoke.

That being said, you probably have an uncle or an aunt in your family who is a heavy smoker and yet has outlived his or her siblings. Why? Because the line of programming code 'smoking = cancer' is absent from their beliefs.

Be careful: before using this argument as an excuse to start smoking again, be absolutely sure that you believe there is no link whatsoever between smoking and health problems. This belief is almost universal in developed nations (and constantly reinforced by medical research and the media), so again I recommend you do not smoke if you are the least bit addicted to cigarettes.

In fact, you should aim at attaining complete neutrality with regard to cigarettes and alcohol. In other words, if a single glass of Scotch pushes you into (or back into) alcoholic addiction, you are as dependent as an alcoholic. Independence here is measured by your capacity to control yourself fully and to stop when you decide to.

• Ejaculation (male and female) is synonymous with orgasm.

This is a really sad belief! Fact: ejaculation for both sexes represents an enormous amount of spent physical and mental energy. You're sceptical? Go ahead, try to get some serious work done after having had three ejaculations in two hours. Get back to me on this! Orgasm and ejaculation can happen simultaneously but do not necessarily happen at the same time. It's another 'ham story'. You can have an orgasm without ejaculating and conserve a lot of energy.

• Parents have a responsibility to educate their children.

This one is worth more attention, and I will come back to it later.

• You can actually help others in life.

Let's suppose you find a little animal hurt by the side of the road. Wanting to help it, you pick it up and put it down in the forest a little ways away, pleased with yourself at having 'helped' it. But how do you know that you did help it? Can you be sure? What if the animal was trying to cross the road to join its family waiting in the bushes on the other side and by 'helping' you just separated the group and made it impossible for the little beast to go where it wanted?

If you really want to help out, start by becoming someone who enjoys life fully, who finds life marvellous, who reaches out and supports others by encouraging them to change their sad and boring lives. But stay away from altruism. True altruism begins with your own personal development. Have you ever seen a blind man guided by a blind seeing-eye dog? I don't think so!

'Pierre, you aren't being realistic.'

I know. But neither are you. Nobody is realistic when they try to explain their personal reality and export it into someone else's life.

So you're right, there's no way I can be realistic in your reality. But I don't want anything to do with your reality. I prefer my own, as crazy as it might seem to you.

So-called 'normal' people work up to seventy hours a week for $40,000 a year, get depressed at age thirty, and have heart attacks at fifty. Frankly, I couldn't be more thrilled to be crazy!

'If only I had . . .'

Did you know that less than 1 per cent of people die happy? That's right. No more than 9 people out of every 1,000 say in the days before their death that they have lived a satisfying life.

Of course, if you ask people in the street, everyone will tell you how satisfied they are with their lives. It's only a facade. The dying, you see, have one advantage: they couldn't care less what you might think of them, so they are much more truthful.

And the regrets they have! So many regrets.

Their mistakes? Oh, no, they don't regret their mistakes.

> What people regret at the end of their lives is not the mistakes they made—it's what they wanted to do but never did.

So how much time do you think you should spend trying to avoid errors, how much time analyzing and studying things to make sure you avoid doing the wrong thing instead of just doing something?

The answer is zero minutes, zero seconds. Not a single iota of our precious time should ever be spent on 'what if' scenarios and analyses. If one sad day, we feel remorseful thinking about all the things we never had a chance to do, it's because of the time we wasted earlier in life trying to plan out things because we were afraid to make mistakes. We should even suppress the whole concept of mistakes and dive into the pool of challenges that we will otherwise, when it's too late, regret not having tackled.

The heck with errors! Anyway, who is to say if something is an error unless he or she can predict the future? How can you honestly say that you have made a mistake until you know where the 'mistake' may lead you?

You haven't got a clue, you see! So ask and you shall receive! But you have to ask, not just ponder!

> Successful people act. People who wish they were successful only think about it.

What is reality anyway?

Each and every one of us has his or her own personal reality. We look at the events of our lives through a lens whose shape, curve, thickness, and colour vary according to the experiences we have. And since there are no two human beings alive with exactly the same collection of beliefs and experiences, each and every life is at its start a blank sheet. And that, in short, is what life is all about: making new paintings, not plagiarizing, cloning, or photocopying another life.

So don't try to be *realistic* in the common meaning of the word. Try to define the reality that will make you most happy, independent of the opinions of others.

In my reality, I can have whatever I desire, spend my time playing (not working), and avoid all responsibilities. In a word, I can simply ask and receive.

Extreme virtual reality

Last summer, on our family trip to Florida, my children and I tried a new game. We were each given a strange-looking helmet to wear. These helmets were equipped with wrap-around glasses that let us experience a fully mobile virtual world, which we controlled by moving our heads.

All of a sudden, we found ourselves in a *Star Wars* world, lightsabres in hand. Our goal was to kill the horrible monsters that came into our field of vision using the lightsabres. (Sorry about the violence.) Even better, our 'suits' allowed us to feel vibrations and small electric shocks whenever one of the drooling two-headed beasts succeeded in attacking us. I was completely captivated, so much so that when our team was destroyed by the huge green monster at the end of the game, I wanted to begin another one immediately.

But what if your life too were no more than a virtual reality? What if your body were only a part of an immense scenario that allowed you to taste and undergo as many new experiences as possible in the sophisticated suit we call the human body?

After the game was over, I got to thinking. The difference between our everyday lives in the human 'suit' and the experience I had just enjoyed in virtual reality was a lot less than many of us might imagine.

A fabulous machine

Listen. This very moment, while you are reading these words, more than five trillion chemical reactions are taking place in your body. That's right, each second of your life! Can you control that? Can you mentally manage all that?

Of course, you can't. But it all takes place anyway in perfect harmony right down to the last little detail without any rational input on your part. But something must be managing it.

And don't come back to me with the theory of random events because if your body (and the whole marvellous universe in which it evolves) were only the product of random events, half the time you would see yourself decomposing right under your nose. *Glug, glug, glug.*

But it doesn't happen! It all works all the time. Everything takes place with unparalleled synchronism without your conscious knowledge, without you controlling any part of it voluntarily.

That's quite a suit you've got there, pal—more evidence that should convince you that you are really on vacation here and that you just have to ask to receive.

Still not on board? Okay, let's go on.

The Albert muscle

Success is, above all, a state of mind, a way of thinking and of tackling your day-to-day existence and the situations it brings.

Take Albert, for example, the most special person I have ever had the pleasure of knowing. First of all, Albert failed his junior college finals seven times in a row—seven years of his life!

At some point, seeing the poor boy fade more and more into the woodwork, his teachers decided to give him an easy three-question test. A single correct answer, and they would recommend that he receive his junior college diploma so he could be admitted to a university for a degree in quantum physics!

The first question they asked Albert was 'How many days of the week begin with the letter *Y*?'

'That's a snap,' Albert replied. 'Just one.'

Their jaws dropped as he finished his answer, 'Yesterday.'

Maybe it wouldn't be that easy to get rid of the boy after all!

'All right, now, question two, and please pay attention. How many seconds are there in a year? You have three hours, all the paper and pencils you need, a pocket calculator, and here, take this laptop too, it might help.'

Albert didn't even blink. 'I don't need all that paraphernalia, gentlemen. I know the answer.'

His teachers were astounded. 'You mean you figured it out just like that?'

'Well, it isn't very hard to calculate. It's obvious the answer is twenty-four.'

There were a lot of unhappy muttering at this, followed by 'What do you mean twenty-four seconds in a year?'

'Sure. There's the second of January and then the twenty-second, the second and twenty-second of February, of March, April, and so on until December. Twelve months, twenty-four *seconds*.'

Generalized groaning broke out at the thought they would be seeing old Albert in all the same classes the following semester.

'Albert, listen up. This is your last chance. How many *T*s are there in "Silent Night"?'

'Boy, that's a real tough one,' Albert replied. 'I think I'll need that laptop now.'

Mystified, his teachers watched Albert retreat to a corner of the room. He hunched over the laptop, muttering and sweating in deep concentration. Finally he smiled, wiped his brow, and came back with his answer.

'There are exactly seven *T*s.'

'What are you talking about, you cretin?' one exasperated professor shrieked. 'There are only two: one in *Silent* and one in *Night*.'

'Oh, no,' replied Albert. 'The Christmas carol goes on, "Holy Night, all is calm, all is bright. Yon young Virgin . . ." It took me a while to remember all the words, but then I counted up all the *T*s, and I'm sure my answer is correct.'

As you might assume, Albert never did receive his degree. But he has become one of the most interesting people I have ever met, succeeding in everything he puts his hand to from business to love.

What is the secret of his success? He just doesn't think like everyone else. Where you might see an obstacle, Albert sees an opportunity. Where you see a problem, he sees a solution.

Everything comes down to your beliefs. You have the Albert muscle too. It might be a little atrophied, but you do have it. So train it!

Three forbidden thoughts

When I give workshops on the laws of success, I always begin by describing three thoughts that no one is allowed to have during the whole process, and I'm going to do the same now with you.

And don't laugh. I'm watching you!

1. It is strictly forbidden to think 'Yeah, he has a few interesting ideas, but I've been looking at life my way for thirty years. There's no way I'm going to change at this point.'

2. It is strictly forbidden to think 'True, what I've been reading so far is interesting, but it doesn't really apply to me. I have constraints that others don't have. My case is unique.' Your case is not unique in the least. Everything you read in this book applies to your own reality. I guarantee it!

3. Finally, it is strictly forbidden to think 'Yes, but . . .' You had better decide, once and for all, whether you're in or you're out—yes or no, no buts.

Do we have a deal?

States of Mind

Right from the start of this book, I have been showing you the path at the end of which you will find the legendary philosopher's stone that the alchemists sought, the key to turning lead into gold. Think of it as a shortcut, one that can transform your apparently humdrum existence into an exciting life.

> What's the secret? Learning how to develop useful beliefs and how to ask the 'universe' for things that a really inspiring life deserves.

This shortcut is really only one of many possible shortcuts. But since I know you prefer more complicated paths—you feel better about it if you have to work hard—let's go for the more rigorous and full-length treatment.

We have to bring your sacrosanct, 'rational' brain to accept—no easy task— that it is not the principal actor in your life. To get there, we're going to follow a well-structured process and undertake an exhaustive treatment of this question.

We will learn the four states of mind that lead to success, the five main enemies we need to confront, and the three most important allies in our exciting quest for paradise on earth.

Then we'll get down to business. Ideas and concepts are great, but unless we do something with them, they're not good for much. Spirituality includes materialism, and there is no need to limit paradise to somewhere that is foreign to the place and space you're in right now. After all, if God exists, he's everywhere.

So let's get to it. We'll start by building your ideal life using a method called the star of dreams.

Then we'll kick into high gear with a review of the seven great laws of the Tao of business and the six most important amplifiers of these laws.

And for the finale, once we're at cruising speed, we'll go through some important practical considerations concerning how to integrate the divine and the magical into your life always using an experimental and scientific philosophy.

> My goal is no less than making you into a better god or goddess.
>
> As long as you have to ask, ask for something big! After all, if we were made in God's image, we might as well affirm it loud and clear and take advantage of it.

The first state of mind: test, test, and test again

If you really want to have an exciting life that is full of adventure and success, you have to approach it scientifically. And, by the way, that does not mean a life without faith. On the contrary, science, far from excluding faith, is the foundation of faith. The greatest obstacle to faith is your intellect's resistance to a concept or a phenomenon that seems irrational from the get-go.

Your faith would quite naturally embrace the proposition I have been suggesting so far, 'ask and you shall receive', if your mind could refrain from rationalizing everything and refusing to believe that almost nobody has an ideal life. So your intellect pigeonholes this idea into a 'symbolic but impractical' slot.

Remember the story of Aristotle and Galileo? Aristotle carried the exclusive use of rational logic to extremes while ignoring faith and experience. While Galileo, by using an experiment with cannonballs of different weights to verify his proposition regarding the speed of falling objects, showed us the enormous importance of an approach to problem-solving based on real experience.

Your challenge will be to call everything about your beliefs into question until you have experimented with every single one of the rules and hypotheses that make up your mindset.

In other words, you have to test these beliefs scientifically.

If someone tells you that you could increase your energy level at work by removing your shoes, you shouldn't start to theorize about it, give your immediate opinion, or attack the principle involved. What you should do is say to yourself, 'Strange idea, probably won't pan out, but I'll give it a try. Let's see if it works for me.'

> From this day forward, become a devoted sceptic. Always tell yourself, 'I'll try it out and see if it works for me.'

Test your ideas, test your principles, test the rules by which you live.

Test the belief that you always have to take your meals at the same time.

Verify what happens when you eliminate the word *no* from your vocabulary and from your kids' lives.

Test what happens when for a whole day, you follow your instincts for no rational reason.

Test what happens when you refuse to have preconceived opinions for seven consecutive days.

Test, test, and test again.

Don't judge, don't analyze, don't reason; for heaven's sake, just give it a try!

The elastic minute

Here's a question for you: what do you know about bungee jumping? You've seen people on TV practising this extreme sport, jumping off towers or bridges with their feet attached to an enormous elastic rope. So you know about bungee jumping? Really?

Don't fall into Aristotle's trap. If you have never bungee-jumped yourself, you don't really know about bungee jumping. All you know about is the concept, not the reality of the sport.

Memorize the following rule:

> I hear, so I forget.
>
> I see, so I remember.
>
> I do, so I understand.
>
> I hear, so I forget.
>
> I do, so I understand
>
> I hear, so I forget.
>
> I see, so I remember
>
> I do, so I understand.

There is only one way to truly know something, and that is to do it, to taste it, to try it out for yourself!

Now tell me truthfully, how many of the principles of your life have you blindly accepted without ever having tested them? Do you take anything and everything at face value just because you saw it on television or because you heard it from a parent, a friend, or your banker?

Let's take an example. Suppose you want to start your own business. You no doubt think that the first steps include preparing a business plan, designing an attractive logo, and having a corporate brochure printed up.

Do you think there might be another way? Will you be surprised to know that the most successful business people did not begin like this?

Here is another example. You probably think that it is better to put money aside before buying something. Yet this flies in the face of the natural law of action and reaction, which has been scientifically proven: the more water pours out one end of a pipe, the more the pipe sucks water in from the other end. This is the principle of the siphon.

It is exactly the same with money: the more goes out, the more comes in. And you can take that to the bank!

The more you block up the pipe, the less water flows. The more money you put aside, the more you block the money pipe. It's obvious, really. How can you have money in front of you if you put it aside?

But be careful. You have to accept the entire equation. You also have to develop a belief in the power of action and reaction. For example, if you start spending wildly and using the action–reaction principle as an excuse without profoundly believing in it, you'll risk making your situation worse.

If each time you spend money, your brain tells you to stop spending money you don't have because your debts will pile up, your banker won't like it, and you'll end up losing everything and becoming homeless. Well then, your negative thoughts will quickly translate into unpleasant financial experiences because in fact that is what you will have asked for. You will have asked for it merely by having thought about the difficult position these new expenses will put you in.

In order for the law of action and reaction to work to your advantage, you have to spend money convinced that the universe will offer you a way to generate the new revenue that you will need to cover the expenses. And obviously, you don't start by buying a half-million-dollar house. You need some training in order to succeed. So start with small purchases.

Now, since faith is built on real experience, let's take a quick test.

Let's suppose you want to buy a new car, but it costs $300 more than your monthly budget can handle. Buy it anyway—that's my advice to you. Go ahead, hurry over to the dealership, buy the vehicle, and watch closely what happens to you during the following forty-eight hours.

You heard me. I repeat, go buy the car before you know how you will be able to make the first payment.

Since the action–reaction principle works at all levels, the reaction to the action of signing the car contract should be simultaneous.

An opportunity will definitely present itself to enable you to generate the funds you need to cover this new expense. When it does, don't reject it, don't analyze it, don't weigh the pros and cons. Just seize the opportunity when it comes. And it will come almost magically as a reaction to the action you took in signing for the automobile.

I know it seems hard to believe. These beliefs weigh us down so much. But I'm telling you, there is an enormous difference between living on credit and living by the scientific principles of action and reaction.

If you live on credit, your spending just increases your stress level, and you spend all your time worrying about what will become of you. And especially, you let the opportunities to make money that pass your way pass you by.

If you live according to the principle of the siphon and of action/reaction, you make your purchase, and simultaneously you seize the opportunity, out of necessity, that presents itself to you to allow you to balance your action. It's a law of the universe. Don't think about it, don't analyze it, just utilize it.

When you let an object drop from your hand, you don't spend time speculating in advance on what may happen to it. You know that gravity exists. The object in question will simply fall to the ground. Well, it is exactly the same for all the laws I talk about in this book. Don't waste time trying to analyze them. Just use them; it's as simple as that.

And remember, the relative length of a minute can be a lot longer or a lot shorter. It just depends on what side of the bathroom door you happen to be on!

➤ The test of the moving finger

Perhaps you don't agree that the more you spend your money instead of saving it, the more opportunities you will find to make even more. The thing is, your opinion in this respect is worthless. Mine too, as it happens.

An opinion is nothing more than a point of view. It's your legitimate right, of course, to hold on to the one you have if it is profitable to you. Nonetheless, your point of view is only one way of looking at things. And there are many, many other ways of looking at things.

Just because the majority of people hold a certain point of view does not mean it represents absolute truth.

Remember Aristotle, and try this: Lift your right arm over your head, and point your index finger towards the sky. Now, using your finger, trace some circles in the air, going clockwise. That's right, go ahead. Make a few more. You're sure you're moving clockwise, right? Absolutely convinced?

Okay, let's verify it. Keeping your finger moving and pointed at the ceiling, lower your hand to the level of your tummy and look at it again. Still moving clockwise? Oops! The finger is going counter-clockwise. Strange but true, and you were so convinced! So how is it that the rotation went from clockwise to counterclockwise when your finger never stopped moving in the same direction?

It's simple. Your point of view changed!

You see the circles traced by your finger from above when it is at the level of your tummy, but from below when it is above your head.

Now tell me, how many realities were there in this exercise? Two? No, there was only one absolute reality, only one movement. But there was an infinite number of relative realities.

Somebody standing ten yards in front of you observing this experiment would have seen neither clockwise nor counterclockwise movement, only movement of your finger from left to right and from right to left. Not convinced? Don't think about it, try it!

> There is only one absolute reality but an infinite number of relative realities.

Once you have accepted as fact that we live in a relative universe, as Einstein so elegantly showed us, then you have to accept the fact that your point of view has exactly the same value as all other points of view and that it is useless to argue about it.

Debates, arguments, opinions—they are all meaningless. The only thing that matters is sharing a point of view—or not.

And this is one of the most important rules you will ever learn. Everyone is always right.

You find life difficult? Well, you are right.

You find life easy? You are right too.

You find everything I'm teaching you ridiculous? Right again!

You see, you are always right within your own point of view.

You find the house is a mess, but your partner finds it orderly. And you are both right. Why bother arguing about it? You observe the same reality but each through a lens curved by your own personal experiences and beliefs.

So if the house is not clean enough to your liking, do something to improve it in your eyes, and leave your partner in peace!

Go ahead and try it out. Stop expecting things from others. Try to simply act according to your own point of view, and let others live by their points of view. You'll be astonished by the results.

So in a word, from now on, learn to say, 'You are right.'

If your point of view is different from that of others, who cares? You'll keep it or abandon it according to the results it brings; it's as simple as that.

You no longer like the influence a certain point of view has on your life? No problem, just change it. Toss it in the trash, and move on to another point of view. If people accuse you of changing your way of thinking as easily as you put on a fresh shirt, you can tell them they are right, that you prefer spanking-clean shirts, and go on your merry way. An opinion uselessly clung to is of absolutely no value.

Just imagine the look on the face of your boyfriend or girlfriend when you announce, 'Sweetheart, I just realized that my opinion is absolutely without value!' You won't have long to wait for this answer: 'Well, you didn't have to read a book to learn that. I've been telling you the same thing for years!'

Duality and opposing couples

Every single experience we have on earth takes place on an axis of opposing couples. You only know something is warm because you have experienced cold. You perceive up because there is down, and there is light because of darkness.

Everything on earth is bipolar—well, almost everything. Let's say that everything your senses perceive has two poles.

Imagine for a second that you have no concept of darkness. How would you conceive of light? Since light would have no opposite, you would never be conscious of its presence. You would never even perceive the fact that you live in an environment of light, and the concept would never make its way into your mind.

If unipolar things exist on earth, we cannot perceive them, at least not with the help of our senses. Trying to explain them would be as difficult as explaining water to a fish.

➢ Good and evil

Man/woman, left/right, hot/cold—all these are pairs of coupled opposites.

'But do you really mean it is impossible for us to recognize good in the absence of evil?'

Just so.

> We would not be free to perceive good if evil did not exist.

God created the universe (just accept the concept for the moment; we can talk more about it later) and left us free to know good. Of necessity then, he allowed evil to exist; otherwise, he would have simply imposed goodness on us all. Good has no value per se and can only give us pleasure insofar as evil is present.

The desire to eliminate evil is equivalent to also eliminating our understanding of good. So you can put a big *X* over your plans for a life of adventure and success if you want to waste time trying to eliminate evil. Evil is an essential component of the trip.

> In the Garden of Eden, there are the roses and the thorns, good and evil. Both are necessary parts of the structure of paradise on earth. Make your choice!

Nobody forces you to spend your whole day among the thorns. Try concentrating on the roses for a change!

Experiment a little with the principle of coupled opposites. Try it; it's going to be very useful to you. Think of the energy you waste worrying about all the evil that exists on earth, all that weight on your shoulders, and for what? Are you happier or more efficient because you worry about the bad news you pick up from television and the newspapers?

In this relative universe of ours, there are, still and all, some clues to the existence of absolute truth. For example, the speed of light is, in our universe, a constant that never seems to change no matter how or from which point of view we observe it. Whether we are in motion or at rest, the speed of light never changes.

How about another constant: happiness. Happiness is an absolute. In fact, happiness has neither a beginning nor an end. It is permanent, a constant, always the same, always perfect.

How could happiness have an opposite? If there was an opposite to it, it would be possible for happiness not to exist. If that were possible, we would not be speaking of happiness but of pleasure.

The coupled opposites that can be the subject of a book about success in this earthly paradise are pleasure and pain, and pleasure and misfortune. Happiness, true happiness, resides far above the plane of these opposites.

So for the moment, let's go forward at full speed on the road to discovering the laws of success and try to maximize your pleasure of living and to minimize your moments of misfortune and pain.

That said, you must accept that, on this earth, we cannot do away with pain. On this earth, if you choose to buy a house, you will have to deal with the 'pain' of having to take care of it and of mowing the lawn and watering the flowers. You choose to have a child? Well, the pain that comes with that choice is the knowledge that one day that child will die.

Pleasure and pain—a coupled pair that cannot be avoided in paradise on earth.

On the other hand, there are no limits to the degree of pleasure that you can experience. Oh, I can already hear you. You think pleasure is a sin, don't you? You have certainly felt guilty at having too much fun. And haven't you also had the impression of being unfair when you work less than some people and yet earn more?

You have to be deprogrammed. The pleasure of living is the reason you were put on this earth. It's also a wonderful way to start your trip towards the absolute state of happiness. But that's another story.

For the moment, it's time to experiment. It's spice-up-your-life time.

The second state of mind: a good nose

According to you, are the most highly successful people rational or intuitive? Said another way, do they make their decisions based mostly on analysis or on instinct?

Well, if you are like most people, you will have replied that successful people rely mostly on their instincts.

Fine.

So tell me, how many hours a week do you spend working on developing your instinct? (And, no, intuition is not just a feminine trait.)

How many hours do we spend exercising, bulking up, developing what we call instinct? I'll tell you: none, zero, zilch.

And yet you spend dozens and dozens of hours developing your rational knowledge: attending classes to acquire a better understanding of various software programs for computers; French, Spanish, or German classes; time management seminars; revolutionary marketing workshops; and I don't know what else.

This just doesn't make any sense!

> If you want to become successful and you know that the most successful people rely first and foremost on their instincts, you have to, first of all, work at developing your instinct.

The same problem is rampant in the education system. Schools, for the most part, are totally focused on developing reason and intellect. So it's hardly surprising that among those people who have the best lives, few have been able to tolerate the school system all the way to graduation. (Or as Mark Twain once wrote, 'I never let schooling get in the way of my education.')

I have a BSc. You too? Worked hard to get it? Well, you'll have to work hard to get over it too! When I think about it, I almost laugh when my kids ask me if they can skip classes on the occasional day.

If one day schools decide first and foremost to teach intuition, instinct, and creativity and put aside report cards, grades, and competition, not only will I make sure my kids attend every class, I'll re-enrol myself! But until then, school is far from being the first priority for me and my children.

I know, I know, I'm not being realistic.

Fired for being 'uncreative'

Did you know that before he worked in the movies and created so many memorable characters (like Mickey Mouse, Donald Duck, and Dumbo) and before he brought Disneyland and Disney World to the children of the world, Walter Disney was a journalist? And did you know that he was let go because his boss didn't think he had enough imagination?

If he lacked imagination, what can you say about his boss?

As soon as Disney let his imagination roam free without worrying about money, things really began to happen. As he himself said, 'If I had listened to my bankers, I would never have succeeded at anything.'

The third state of mind: keeping a mental age of four

If I was to ask you to tell me who has the most fun in life, you'd probably point to kids, especially young kids.

If you have ever held a child in your arms, well, you know what a sense of indescribable joy children project. What we sense from them is in fact a kind of innocence untainted by doubt, worries, stress, and remorse.

And they have no past or any memory. Their only connection is to the present.

If you really want to achieve a magical life, go back and find in you that mental age of four. Bring alive the spontaneity, the joy of living for the moment, without worrying what the neighbours might think.

Jesus said, 'Bring to me the little children, for the kingdom of heaven belongs to them.' Notice he said 'belongs' and not 'will belong'. Heaven exists right here on earth. But to get past the gate, you have to be childlike or, more to the point, to think like a child.

How many four-year-olds do you know have put money aside for tomorrow or have a pension fund or a retirement investment account?

Has your little girl ever come to you and said, 'Dad, I don't know what's come over me. I feel so guilty at having spilled that glass of milk yesterday at the restaurant. I just know I'll never feel good again. I think I really need to see a psychologist.'

Have you ever seen your little boy filling in his Daytimer or looking at his daily to-do list?

I doubt it. Children spontaneously live in the present. The past, the future—none of it means anything to them, at least not until we intelligent adults cram these stupid concepts down their throats, such as in the following scenario:

'Go to bed, you have school tomorrow.'

'But, Dad, I'm not sleepy.'

'Doesn't make any difference. Just go to bed.'

'But why?'

'It's better for you, that's all.'

That's all! We train them to sleep more than they need to when they are young. And when they grow up, when they're thirty, forty, or fifty, they'll try to reduce the time they spend sleeping. Now that's what I call really sensible!

What do you think happens in the mind of a child when we order them not to listen to their bodies but follow the unjustified orders of their parents?

The child begins to live in a world of artificial concepts rather than in the real world. He begins to learn to spend his waking hours regretting the past and planning for the future. He learns about concepts like yesterday and tomorrow.

And yet, kids fortunately have the ability to show us the way in the twinkling of an eye. The other day, for example, my little girl innocently asked me, 'Daddy, why do I have to go to bed when Mom is the one who is exhausted?'

Well . . . just because.

Who should educate whom?

Here are a few more questions I'd like to toss your way. (I can't help it. After all, the book is entitled *Ask and You Shall Receive*, and it just so happens I ask a lot.)

Is evolution moving us forward or backward, for example? 'Forward!' I hear you say. Fine. Excellent. In that case, who do you think should be the teachers and who the students?

Because if evolution moves us forward, it follows that we are more evolved than our parents and our children more evolved than us.

Let's be logical. Now is the time for rationality. Our children should be teaching us and not vice versa! My kids are my most precious teachers, my most divine gurus.

> Madness is hereditary; we inherit it from our children.

What are my children teaching me? To disengage myself from my problems, free my mind from my complexes, and concentrate on laughter and play.

One recent evening, I was talking with my long-suffering and valorous wife, Jessy, going on and on about how the project I was working on was proceeding too slowly. Meanwhile, on the other side of the room, our three kids (Charlie, nine years old; Timmy, five; and Jaimee, just eight months old) were observing us. We were frowning, but they were in the midst of gleeful laughter. Timmy had just figured out that he could make Jaimee laugh hysterically by dropping a little bag that made the sound of a fart when it hit the ground.

Our discussion became more and more twisted while their laughter became louder and louder. Finally, I looked at my wife, smacked my forehead with the palm of my hand, and cried out, 'There they go again, bringing us right back to the here and now.'

We got down on the floor, joined the party, and the rest of our evening was spent in an uncontrollable farting hilarity.

The next morning, the phone rang, and I learned that the problem that had seemed so vexing the previous evening had solved itself during the night. I thanked heaven for my kids . . . and for the fart bag!

Play comes before everything else, even before learning

I don't want to spend too much time talking about kids, but since they symbolize to me the door to paradise, I'd like to throw a few more observations your way.

Most children need to move around to feel good. But most schools punish restlessness and oblige kids to sit still at a desk all day long in order to be 'taught'. It's no surprise that our children automatically conclude that learning is a boring business.

A child has to learn first and, above all, to play, play, play, and play again. Sooner or later, from the child's play will come the natural development of an interest in something. From inside himself, he will learn what he needs to do to realize his role on this earth—but not until he fulfils his need to play.

The universe is infinitely intelligent. Each life form has a precise role to play in it. Left to themselves, children will rapidly find their place. But imposing the constricting rules of adults on children just forces them to conform to a mould that probably doesn't fit. Listen to the Pink Floyd song 'The Wall' for more on that subject.

Contrary to what most parents believe, I would be highly worried if my kids' playroom and bedroom were not a mess. It's only those adults with unresolved issues concerning order and discipline who feel obliged to impose their artificial rules on their kids.

Try this experiment on for size: Let your kids do whatever they want for two weeks. Keep your boss mentality under wraps and see what happens. 'You feel like running around outside naked, hon? No problem. If it's fun, maybe I'll do it too!'

If you don't teach them what freedom means, where will they learn self-confidence and how to take a decision when they're forty-five, sitting around the table of a management workshop?

Once you allow them to live in freedom, you will also stop using them as servants. If you want a glass of water or a beer, you'll get up and go serve yourself. Just because you brought them into this world doesn't mean they have to be your slaves.

Your kids are very conscious of the risk you took (and the reward you deserve) by accepting them into your life. Don't worry, they'll return the favour eventually.

As far as the rest goes, try to master the laws of success for your own sake and give your children the space they need to find their own roles. If they see you living happily and successfully, they'll quickly follow your lead.

Two mental torturers: memory and time

Life, all of it, takes place in the present.

The force of memory is so great that it constantly destroys the present moment you are living in, a moment that will never come back.

Look, we're all going to die. This means you too! So why get all hot and bothered about it? Is that the worst thing that can happen to you?

Okay, the cat's out of the bag. You're afraid of death, the worst thing. But stop worrying because, listen, *you are going to die one day*! Just accept it once and for all and throw your stress into the trash can because whatever you do, I guarantee it will one day happen.

Now, take all your history and toss it overboard. There it goes—finished, over, won't come back. You can start with a fresh page in front of you. And the page is blank except if you have soiled it with the dark ink of your past.

Your past only exists in your mind.

Do you know how much time it takes for you to have everything that you want from life, success, enjoyment . . . whatever you want from this incredible paradise on earth?

A single second. That's right. Snap your fingers, and you're there!

It's all in your head. You can be a millionaire in a fraction of a second. Accept it. That's all it takes. Okay, snap. Now, you are rich! Welcome to the millionaires' club.

How does it feel?

Ah, if only it were that easy.

So let's move on.

We're working on building up your faith, right? And since your intellect is still clamouring for proof, let's try another experiment. As we have already learned, theories are useless; the only thing that matters is experience.

For the next four weeks, put away your agenda, and remove your watch. Oh, it looks good on your wrist. Is it a fashion statement? Okay then, just take out the battery. Forget that time even exists, and as if you were a four-year-old child, live in the here and now.

'But my work, my appointments, I'll never be on time—'

No buts, no excuses. Do we have a deal or not?

You'll work it out. Isn't this what you want, the life of your dreams? So from now on, there is no future or any past. The future is chosen by you at this very moment by virtue of the thoughts you choose to have right now.

When you bind yourself to an agenda and a schedule, you force yourself to respect a certain path. But who is to say if that particular way of getting from point A to point B is the best one for you? To know that, you would have to be a seer, but you're not.

All you can do is choose point B as best you can and fix your mind on what's happening right now, keeping your mind alert and your senses on full blast.

Living by relying on the past is a lot like driving a car by looking into the rear-view mirror. Whether you steer your life by keeping your eyes on that mirror (the past) or by following a road map (the future), you'll end up in the same place as the car—in the fields of regret!

The fourth state of mind: mental Teflon

Now that we have gone through testing, intuition, and the four-year-old mental age, we are at the last of the four states of mind: the bulletproof mentality.

Since more than 99 per cent of all people die unhappy, it's obvious that there is something seriously wrong with the way most of us live our lives. But if you take a different path, the famous road less travelled, you'd better be ready for the criticism . . . and the adulation.

It will be either one or the other. Some people will call you crazy. Others will idolize you. You might be a god or a devil, but you'll be nothing in between.

> You have to arm yourself with a protective layer that will keep you totally indifferent to both criticism and compliments.

You see, if you have a need for compliments, you have a dependency on others. And if criticism makes you wince, you won't have the inner strength and the will to get where you want to go.

So you mustn't care about what others think, not a whit, zero, zilch, nada.

It's a bit harsh, but it's absolutely true. Think about movie stars or Celine Dion or Donald Trump.

But here's a point: not caring about what others think is not the same thing as not caring about others. It won't make you abusive. It does not mean you aren't sensitive to the well-being of your friends, family, workmates, or members of your congregation.

It just means that you don't worry about their opinions on the way you choose to live.

The elevator test

You want to see if you have a Teflon mentality?

Try this experiment: Next time you take the elevator, change your behaviour. Instead of doing like everyone else (e.g. entering, turning around, and looking at the floor buttons), just go in and don't turn around. Keep facing the rear of the elevator with your back to the closing doors. Now look at the other people around you with an ear-to-ear grin on your face.

What do you think will happen? They'll all lower their eyes and look at their shoes!

If you can do it, you'll have passed the test. But will you dare try? One thing is for sure: if you have the mental age of a four-year-old, you'd do it without hesitating a second.

Let me put it this way: If this simple little exercise gives you the willies, just try to imagine what you'll have to endure when you inform everyone that you will only be living in the present from now on; that you have finally decided to ask to get what you want; that you're no longer going to put money aside; that you're putting the power of the law of action and reaction to work for you and that you're no longer going to make any plans; that your kids are going to be in charge of educating you from now on; and that you have no more retirement savings account, no insurance, and no pension; oh, and that you are meditating to connect to the universal collective brain!

If you look at it this way, the elevator test is a walk in the park.

The Five Enemies of Success

We're going to turn our attention to the enemies of success. First, though, I strongly recommend that you get into the habit of regularly practising the four states of mind covered in the previous section of the book, concentrating your energy on each one in turn.

For example, you could decide to use the first week of each month to test one of your current beliefs and replace it with a more useful one as needed.

During the second week of each month, you could work on developing your intuitive abilities and your instinct.

The third week of each month could be devoted to the world of children. Jump into it, play with kids, spend time with them, lose your watch and your appointment book, and live only in the present.

And the final week of each month could be devoted to the development of your mental Teflon. You could use this week to test your audacity and your sensitivity to criticism or your dependence on the compliments of others.

If you assimilate this new discipline into your day-to-day existence, you will quickly come to see substantive changes in your life and in the way others see you.

Of course, people will also call you crazy, but that in itself is a sign of progress!

Now, pay attention. We're about to get into serious business—the enemies of success. It might be better to go off by yourself for the next little while so that you can read what follows without interruption. These enemies are powerful, terribly strong, and understanding them will require all your attention.

So paper and pencils, please!

The origins of the enemies of success

Before we get down to brass tacks, let's look at where success's enemies come from in order of importance.

> You, yourself, are the biggest enemy of your own success.
>
> That's right, you—you and your beliefs.
>
> But you're in luck because you have in your hands this book, which is dedicated to teaching you how to master your own thoughts.

Second in importance: your spouse. Your husband or your wife, probably the closest person in the world to you, has an enormous impact on your decisions in life. At the risk of shocking you, I have to say that you must make your life decisions as if your partner were not even there. And you'll need a lot of mental Teflon to get by that one!

Think about it. If your partner—wait, break that word down: *part-ner*. A *part-ner* can't be completely in your life, only *part-ly* in your life. With all the *part-ial* promises and part-ial commitments, it's not surprising that so many marriages fall *a-part* and that so many of us are paying a part of their revenue in alimony to their ex-partners.

But if your life partner truly loves you, he or she will let you be who you are and do what makes you happy. And if you do what makes you happy, your life will shine, money will come all by itself, and you can enjoy a vibrant life together. It really is that simple!

If you want to live in a happy couple relationship, step-by-step compromise will not lead you there. Compromise only creates not one but two unhappy partners, two individuals who don't have what they had hoped for in any particular situation.

Now for the source of the third enemy of success: the family itself. Your brother-in-law's sarcasm, your mother-in-law's jealousy, the unsolicited snarky comment from your grandfather—these come at you from all sides, and each and every member of your tribe will have a word to say about your life and your choices. The best solution is silence, and don't forget the mental Teflon.

The source of the fourth enemy of success is your work environment, i.e. your colleagues. Think about it. Your workmates haven't much real interest in seeing you succeed and rise above the crowd. When you succeed, it only makes them feel guilty at having lacked the courage to take the steps that could lead to their own success. How much easier it is for them to try to slow you down by sowing the seeds of self-doubt.

And, finally, enemy number five: society.

Do you read the newspapers, watch the news on TV? What are you anyway, a masochist? How many murders, rapes, or wars do you have to look at to become motivated to do something every day to improve your life?

You, your partner, your family, your workmates, and the society at large are in declining order of importance at the root of the enemies of success. The golden rule here is to keep quiet about what you do and behave as if you were the guard dog of your own thoughts.

Now, let's look at these enemies in detail.

Enemy number 1: fear

My own point of view, which stems from my research, is that fear is the most dangerous enemy of success. But at the same time, fear can be a precious resource for us. Think about it for a minute. The more dangerous something is to us, the more it obliges us to look into ourselves to understand ourselves better and comprehend why it is dangerous.

The simple voicing of the word *fear* generates fear. If someone asks you if you are afraid, you will react strongly because the word itself is highly charged with significance.

If somebody asks you if you like French fries, you'll hardly lift an eyebrow. But the word *fear* is oh so much more of a menace than the innocuous fry (except my wife's—no, never mind; I'm too attached to my married income tax deductions to open that can of worms).

But where does fear come from? What brings it on? Let's take a look at what happens when you open the door of your mind and let this monster in. You stiffen up, become hesitant, troubled, and everything becomes sombre and blocked up. Fear constricts the circulation of your blood, your thoughts, and the movement of life.

But everything in this universe of ours moves. Nothing, absolutely nothing, remains static. Even this book you hold in your hands is in motion even if the particles that it is made of are oscillating at such enormous speeds that you have the impression of holding a fixed object.

But it does move.

It moves much like the spokes of a wheel that has attained a certain rotational speed. When we observe the wheel as it turns, we sometimes have the impression that it is motionless because its cadence has become synchronized with the frequency of our eyes, just as in the movies, where the fixed images projected on the screen come alive in well-calculated, well-timed movement.

If fear blocks this movement of life, it is the sworn enemy of the relative world. But that said, why are we afraid—and of what?

What we know and what we don't know

The traditional answer to this question is, we fear the unknown.

Sorry, I don't buy it. I respect that point of view, but I can't agree. How can I be afraid of what I don't know?

> I don't fear the unknown at all. What I fear is losing the known, and that's where the expression 'I have nothing to lose' comes from. When we realize we haven't much that is known to lose, the fear of the unknown evaporates.

That's the secret of vanquishing our fears: having nothing to lose!

But you're thinking, 'How can I have nothing to lose when I have a house (mortgage to pay), children (to feed and raise), and work (to get done)?'

Let me remind you that, in any case, whether you want to or not, sooner or later you will lose everything. Your trip to this paradise called earth will one day expire. You weren't given a one-way ticket.

So put all the parts of the equation together. You will lose everything at the time of your death, which could occur some years from now or in an hour. Plus, when that time is close, you will regret all the things you never dared to do.

What does this mean? Live as if you have nothing, and dare to try everything!

If you have nothing, you won't fear to lose what you know, and the fear that holds you back will disappear.

Your children are not your property. They come from you, but they do not belong to you.

Your body doesn't really belong to you either because you don't really control it, not completely—in fact, only a very little bit. As I have explained, while you are reading these very lines, more than five trillion chemical reactions per second occur in your body.

So if your body doesn't really belong to you, what does? Your thoughts perhaps? Maybe.

So in conclusion, you have nothing. And it feels great! Doesn't it open wide the doors of freedom? The heavy weight has been lifted from your shoulders. You own nothing, and in the end, you have no real responsibilities.

You have nothing, so really all you have to lose is your time. Get moving, right now! That project you've wanted to accomplish for years, do it; that new home you thought too expensive, make an offer on it and see what happens; call up someone who turned you on the other day and doesn't even know it; go see your father with whom you've been on non-speaking terms for the last ten years; visit the country you've wanted so much to see with your own eyes and not just on the Internet. Go ahead, do it. Start living right now!

When do you really feel 'good'?

If I was to ask you to describe a moment when you felt really good, what would you say?

Take a pencil and paper, and write down your reply. Be precise. It's the details I want, and lots of them.

Not that easy, is it?

'Well, Pierre, I feel really good when I'm out playing golf.'

Okay. Now tell me why you feel good when you are out on the green. Is it because you hope to hit a really good shot, the feeling when your drive is as good as Tiger Woods's? Is it the sun, the beauty of the course, the nineteenth hole, the way your body relaxes after the game?

Put down in precise detail what makes you feel so good.

> If you ask yourself this question, you will sooner or later conclude that you feel good when your entire mind is living completely in the present.

Golf is not the source of the sense of well-being and harmony (especially when your smirking partners watch your chip shot fall into the water trap).

The source is the permission you give yourself to free up your mind by concentrating solely on that little ball—just for a moment.

The present moment

Losing yourself in the present allows you to eliminate fear.

Take, for example, people who participate in extreme sports. Why would any sane person risk everything he or she has (family, job, money) to perch on the edge of a cliff, jump out of a plane, or dive fifty feet beneath the waves to swim with the sharks?

Why, indeed? To give themselves the freedom of the instant, the here and now. As you prepare to jump off a fifty-foot tower with an elastic band attached to your ankles as all that separates you from a rendezvous with eternity, believe you me, you are not thinking about your month-end car payment or next year's tax return.

One of the most powerful ways to destroy the magic of the moment is learning to name things. The day we teach a child the name of a flower is the day he or she ceases to see that flower because now the concept of the flower has entered his or her memory.

From then on, every time the child sees that kind of flower, it is no longer a new flower for him. He scans his plant concept memory bank, and lo and behold, up pops the name on his mind screen: 'That's a hollyhock.'

It might indeed be a hollyhock, but never before has the child seen that particular hollyhock. So abandon the abstraction, and look at the flower in front of your eyes!

➢ The next restaurant

I have a lot of problems with the future. I can't stand hearing people talk about it. Oh, I love to cook up ideas and projects, but I hate plans and schedules.

When I talk about a project, I do it in the present tense because it already exists in my mind. You see, I know that if I give the project life in my mind, the universal law will take charge of materializing it. That's the way it is.

Why? Because it's a law. Don't analyze it, don't ask why, don't cut it up into little pieces to try to understand it. It's a law of the universe. Period. So just use it!

There is no real difference between a thought, which is a wave of conscious energy, and matter. No real difference at all. 'So', you say, 'how is it that things don't just materialize before our very eyes as soon as we think about them?'

Because there is not enough energy. It's that simple. Einstein taught us that $E = mc^2$. Do you have any idea at all of the quantity of energy necessary for something to materialize? In a simple piece of blackboard chalk, there is enough energy to supply the city of New York with electricity for a whole year!

In order for a thought to materialize and, more to the point, to materialize quickly, it has to be maintained in your mind, and you have to be filled with energy. Each doubt, each worry, each little feeling of fear siphons the creative energy from your thoughts.

Back to the present. Not so long ago, I ate lunch in a restaurant with a friend who began to tell me how he needed to make a lot of money. Oblivious to the excellent food on the table, he didn't even stop talking for a second to smell the tantalizing aroma coming from the plates or taste the delicious food or appreciate the original presentation of the meal.

'What do you want the money for?' I asked him.

'If I had a lot of money, I could finally do what I like, take the time to really live, take advantage of what life has to offer, take my friends on vacation, and enjoy life. I could go to great restaurants and . . .'

And take the time to taste the food maybe?

Stop wasting your life planning a future that you think would allow you to take advantage of the instant you're living in right now.

Money, money, money

Who thinks more about money than someone who has a lot of it? Someone who doesn't have enough of it! The rich are not maniacal about money. The poor are. In fact, the poor think about nothing else.

People who think the most about money are the same ones who tell us that money is the root of all evil.

I don't care for this point of view. Money is just a fluid, a flux that allows you to maximize the diversity of your experience and your adventures in life.

If you really want to live an extraordinary life, you'd better learn to like money. Even better, you're going to have to let money be your partner, your true associate. You'll even have to learn to take it for granted that the money you need is always there next to you in abundance and always available at the right time.

You'll have to convince yourself that it is easy—really, really, easy—to make money. Money is not earned; it is not merited. It's just accepted. So go ahead, accept it.

Money comes along automatically with your stay on this paradise called earth. It's part of the all-inclusive trip you were offered.

➤ Jesus was a millionaire

You must have heard this saying: it is harder for a rich man to go through the hole in a camel's back than—no, wait, I've got it wrong. It is harder for a rich man to enter paradise than for a camel to go through the eye of a needle.

There you go! No better excuse for saying that money is evil and leads you straight to hell. You want my point of view on hell? (You're going to get it anyway.) Hell is living in a three-and-a-half-room apartment with four kids and a second job, working night and day, and not knowing if you'll have enough money for the grocery bill. That's hell to me!

Being rich, according to the Bible, is being satisfied. When you are completely satisfied with what you have, you are no longer hungry for anything. You become static, inactive, morose, and depressed.

Being poor, now, that means wanting more—more experience, more adventure, more freedom, more love, more creativity, more spice in your life.

> As long as you are continually thinking about money—criticizing it, managing it, protecting it, being jealous of those who have lots of it—money will be your Lord.
>
> If money is constantly on your mind, you are its slave, and it is your master.

But if money is only a tool to be used and you use it that way, it loses its power over you. By the way, did you know that Jesus was a millionaire?

Pierre Morency

What other description could there be of a man who could make what he needed appear whenever and wherever he needed it? That's really being rich to my way of thinking. Jesus, a poor carpenter? Don't make me laugh.

➢ How you react to money

I'm going to give you some homework for tonight (that's right, in addition to what you already have). After all, you're the one who asked for details and a well-structured recipe for success. Let me remind you of the simple and direct method: ask and you shall receive.

So I want you to write down in detail and sincerely what you think about money.

- What are your feelings about money?

- What do you believe about wealth?

- Do you believe you have to manage your money?

- Do you believe you have to control it?

- Do you believe it is finite?

- Do you feel you have the right to be rich?

- Would you feel comfortable tomorrow if you won the lottery and found your name and your photograph on the front page of the newspaper?

- Would you feel comfortable about owning a Porsche or guilty about having too much money?

- Are you always afraid of not having enough money?

- When you go to a restaurant or on vacation, do you always choose economically so as to keep some money for later on in life?

Go on, let all the money demons out and write them down. They are the source of all your financial fears, and they are squeezing off your access to the economic fluidity you need to be successful. Come on, write! This is an absolutely fundamental exercise.

You know what millionaires say? 'Nothing but the best, and forget the rest.'

➤ The end-of-the-month thrill

Here is a concrete example of the self-defeating attitude some people have with respect to money.

The end of the month is looming. You know that on the first of the month, you have to take care of the rent, the insurance, the interest on your line of credit, the minimum payments on your credit cards, plus the electricity and telephone bills. The problem is, you're $548 short to pay all these bills.

You're worried. You have an argument about it with your partner. How are you going to get out of this hole?

You're really in a trap. But you know what? You love it!

That's right, and don't try to tell me it isn't true. You love the desperate worry of wondering how you'll meet your obligations so that you can tell yourself afterwards, 'Yes! I did it again!' You love putting yourself in peril so you can take up the challenge of digging yourself out of the mess. You actively seek this feeling, crave the adrenalin that puts some spice into your life. In short, you dig your own hole, throw yourself into it to try to see how you'll ever get out, and all of it for the simple pleasure that getting out of the mess gives you.

Am I wrong? Am I? Then explain to me why you keep playing the end-of-the-month game if it has lost its appeal? Once you decide that this game has lasted long enough, this situation will disappear from your life.

Why not use your energy and enthusiasm to create new scenarios, such as 'What can I do to make $100,000 next month?' Impossible? What do you mean, impossible? Just give it a try, for heaven's sake! Don't take yourself out of the race before the starter's pistol has even been fired.

At least give yourself the chance to play at 'Let's act as if it were possible.'

Okay, okay, so it's impossible. But how would you behave if it were possible? Let's make a 'what if' game out of it, a riddle to be answered.

Invent unrealistic challenges for yourself, and play at submitting them all to your brain for consideration. Sleep on it, take long walks, and see what your unconscious comes up with to solve these new mind twisters.

You will see that the bigger the question is, the bigger the answer will be. It's as we said earlier: the good old principle of action and reaction.

Small demand, small answer; big demand, big answer. You don't have to look any further because it's just as simple as that.

And don't try to read between the lines. There is nothing between the lines!

Enemy number 2: security

These days, you can't take three steps without somebody offering you some kind of protection—insurance over here, savings plan over there, a safety belt, an alarm system. Is there an insurance agent out there who can sell me a policy against insurance agents?

Oh, you want to be rational about it? Okay, let's be rational.

First of all, if you want to protect yourself adequately from all dangers, you have to know all the parameters against which protection is needed, right? So you have to know all the risks of accident, sickness, bankruptcy, electrocution, and I don't know what else.

And yet, the people who live the best lives are undeniably those who are the most comfortable with insecurity.

> You'll have to learn to live being at ease with insecurity. 'Because they neither sow nor reap, yet the Heavenly Father feeds them.'

Think what you like about this, but believe me, it really works. And if I have to choose between counting on the Heavenly Father and an insurance company, I have no doubt about where I'll place my bet.

You think I'm naive? That's your right. But judge the results, not the apparent logic. Look at your own life and name the five most beautiful moments you have experienced.

Go ahead, write them down.

Aren't these moments the ones where you threw caution to the wind and said 'The hell with it, I'm taking the chance' or 'Whatever happens, I'm going for it'? So if throwing caution to the wind brought you the best experiences of your life, why lose that exquisite reflex by burying it under dozens and dozens of layers of protective measures?

Never forget that the greatest fortunes have always been built on risk-taking.

The most beautiful moments of life also stem from risk-taking. You can't keep emergency exits open when you choose to have a child or start a business. You put all your eggs in the same basket.

When I meet with entrepreneurs or professional people in difficult situations, I often perceive that they have ceased to behave as they did when they started out, when everything was working well. They have stopped taking risks and have begun to protect their capital. Their attitude has changed from 'Let's go for it' to 'Let's just hold on to what we have.'

And instead of continuing to enrich themselves, they have begun to enrich their lawyers.

The little shampoo bottles

The need for security is so deeply rooted in our day-to-day existence we can't even see any more how it fills us with fear.

Here's an example: The last time you went to a hotel, don't tell me you refrained from putting all the tiny soap bars, moisturizing lotion, and shampoo bottles into your suitcase to take back home! (Be honest!) And don't tell me you don't already have at least fifty of these samples lying around in one of your bathroom or bedroom drawers just in case nuclear war is declared and you suddenly have an irresistible urge to wash your hair or cream up your skin at that very moment!

And how do I know this? Well, I may have begun to master the universal laws of success, but I too had to climb that same mountain. And I still have lots of tiny shampoo bottles and soaps at the back of my own bedroom and bathroom drawers!

Is it medicine or drugs?

I know the money you put aside for the future is really important to you.

I know your pension plan is really important to you.

I know that people tell you (I admit I was the same, for heaven's sake!) to plan for a life expectancy of fifteen years after retirement, which means you will need $1,253,563 in the bank to bring you an annual revenue of $43,548 without breaking the capital, and to do this, you'll need to put aside $532 a week if you start at age of forty-three, $343 if you start at thirty-five, and only $122 a week if you start saving at the tender age of twenty.

It can get worse. They might tell you it's already too late for you but that you should convince your children to immediately begin planning for their retirement. I know all about it, you see, because I've been down that road, a ways.

But how will you ever be able to put aside $343 a week at age thirty-five when you have to pay the mortgage and upkeep on the house and take care of clothes, furniture, appliances, food, the car, entertainment, the whole shebang?

There is only one way to succeed at it, and that is to build your own enterprise and be successful.

But if you start your own business and it is successful, you won't need your pension plan or your RRSP because you'll have invested your money right at that very moment in yourself and in your own project and you shall receive a much better return on the money than you could ever get from a pension plan.

> The facts are clear. Wealthy people have invested all their resources in their own development and their own projects—not in mutual funds, life insurance, or self-directed RRSPs, but in their own lives!

Investigate for yourself and draw your own conclusions. If you absolutely require security in order to survive, arm yourself every which way, but be forewarned, the line between drugs and medicine is very thin.

If you want to make God laugh, make plans

'A plan here, a plan there, plans everywhere while my life drifted away, carried off by the current . . .'

Why do you insist on fighting the way of the universe?

If the Creator (the 'real you') had wanted you to make plans, he would have given you the power to comprehend the incalculable number of variables needed to be taken into account for any intelligent plan to be successful.

Since we do not know the future (and, between us, it's a lot more fun that way), we should not lose a single minute planning it. Let me remind you, what you will regret at the end is the time lost, not the mistakes made.

Ralph Waldo Emerson once wrote, 'Succeeding in life is succeeding in the next hour.'

If you insist on making plans, limit them to the next sixty minutes, and your life will become simply wonderful.

➤ Oxymorons

The term *oxymoron* refers to a combination of words that are contradictory. The word itself is of Greek origin. The words and expressions we use can cause us problems by increasing our conditioning with respect to, among other things, our need for security.

For example, the expression *marketing plan*, which is so common that it has become a part of linguistic office furniture, leads us to believe that you can't do marketing without a plan.

The expression *financial independence* conditions us to believe that we can be simultaneously independent and in the service of money. My own view is that the more important finance becomes in our lives, the more we are dependent upon it.

Oxymorons are not only prevalent in security-related topics. They are all over the place, and here are a few choice examples (I leave you to decipher what they all mean):

- business plan
- balanced portfolio
- happy retirement
- need of love
- honest politician (oops, I better stop here).

➢ Vision, definitely; plans, no way!

There is a fundamental difference between a vision and a plan.

Of course, you need a vision of what you want. And this vision needs to be precise. In order to ask, you have to want something that is well defined.

Most companies boast about having a vision. But a catchphrase like 'Becoming the North American market leader in the heat pump industry' is not a vision. It's only a sentence designed to please a banker! (I'm not irate here, just intense.)

A vision concerns the complete development of an image that describes the desired goal; it's about seeing.

> It's the same for everything you want from life. You need a clear and complete vision of your desires. Knowing what one wants, moreover, is one of the most difficult things for a human being to master.

71

Once you have a well-defined image, you can keep it in your mind and follow the path of events that will present themselves to you to take you where you want to go.

Of course, you can develop hypotheses about following that road and what you will need along the way, but the stronger your faith is, the less preliminary organization you'll need to do.

Whether it is a question of building an enterprise or climbing a mountain, the degree of preparation and planning is inversely proportional to the level of your faith in yourself.

Ideally, you should only need to select the picture you desire and then let the road to it appear before you by keeping your spirit in the present moment.

Enemy number 3: overprotection

The adjacent enemy to fear and the need for security is overprotection. This shouldn't surprise you as they are all related, which leads you to want to protect everything for fear of having others steal your ideas, your profits, even your business itself.

Well, first of all, they aren't really your ideas, are they? When an idea comes into your mental field of vision, do you really believe you are its creator?

If you think about it differently, you are just a conduit, a channel, a vehicle required to improve the welfare of the human race and all the inhabitants of this planet; if you think about it this way, you will lose the need to protect yourself.

Tell yourself that if the idea came from a source outside your own brain, eventually other ideas will come along from the same origin too.

By grasping on to the first idea that comes along as if your life depended on it, falling under the spell of the catastrophe salesmen, and spending all your money on patents, lawyers, and contracts, you'll end up with nothing, nothing more than an expensive piece of paper sitting on a shelf and a prototype covered with dust.

Not only will your idea never come to fruition or contribute to the improvement of the life of the society around you, but you will have put yourself in financial straits dozens of times for no good reason.

A recalcitrant orthodontist

I can't tell you the number of entrepreneurs, inventors, and creative people who have come to me, saying, 'Pierre, I've come up with the invention of the century. It's worth millions. Can you help me market it?'

It always makes me think of the orthodontist who invented a new way of correcting a problem children have with their palate. A well-disciplined man, he invested all his professional revenue in the development of his system. When the prototype was ready, he followed the advice of his lawyer, who counselled him, of course, to protect himself as quickly as possible by registering a patent on it.

Our courageous inventor put his capital on the line again and patiently waited three years for his patent, which would surely allow him to be bought out by a rich Japanese investor on the lookout for miraculous new ideas.

But there was a worm in the apple. While he was waiting, an American company began selling an apparatus that was surprisingly—a little too surprisingly in fact—similar to his own. The Americans quickly turned a tidy profit, while the orthodontist, who had spent so much trying to protect his invention, had practically no money left.

So what should he have done?

My own take is that he should have brought his invention to market with an outrageous sense of urgency to take advantage of the fruits of his idea before it went out of date. After all, technology moves so quickly these days. Three years of waiting for the patent to be granted, and when it is—bam!—the concept is no longer valid.

The orthodontist's lawyer had a different suggestion: take the Americans to court, naturally overlooking the fact that the US company had made hundreds of thousands of dollars in profit while his client was working day and night to pay for his failed overprotection.

You can guess how it ended.

Overprotection is just as much a problem in the world of contracts. I am and will always remain an ardent believer in the power of the handshake agreement.

Universal justice

Do you believe the world is unjust? Not me.

To the contrary, everything I have observed has shown me just how much the universe is perfectly fair.

Each and every one of us always receives exactly what we ask for. You live the exact life you asked for and that which you go on asking for each and every day. The law of action and reaction (Newton's third law) makes it understood that everything you do will inevitably come back to you.

> Human justice has limits. Universal justice is infinite.

If you accept this principle and are sincere when you say 'You reap what you sow', you must completely submit to the existence of universal justice.

You won't need contracts or patents, and there will be no need to measure if what you have received is in the right proportion to what you think you deserve.

Have faith in the universe. The universe is the best banker, the best accountant, and the best lawyer you could ever hope to hire.

The only true justice has to take into consideration all the events set in motion by any particular act, not just the visible events.

Justice does not depend on the hours of labour put in nor the amount of effort invested; it only depends on the impact of your actions.

If, by a single word, you inspire someone who, because of this inspiration, goes on to invent a technology that brings food and energy to the peoples of the earth, your single word would be worth millions of dollars.

The contrary is just as true. If a hurtful word puts someone in a perilous situation and stops him or her from playing a role that could have contributed to the improvement of the welfare of thousands of others, that debt is entered in your file.

How do you explain that some people are born handicapped, others poor, and still others rich and talented? I call it justice.

But you don't like this answer. And you may not like it at all when I say that everything can be easily explained if you accept the fact of reincarnation.

A church that wants to control your life will tell you that reincarnation does not exist, filling you with the fear of eternal hell. Because if reincarnation did exist, you could tell yourself that you will have another chance at success if things don't work out in this life and refuse to submit to religious authority whose intolerance is in reverse proportion to the size of its ever-shrinking flock.

Haven't you ever given a second chance to your kids or to a friend who has done you wrong? Wouldn't it be only logical that we could also have 'other chances' when we need them?

Besides, all religions in fact support the notion of reincarnation. 'Religions' is what I said, not 'religious organizations'. To convince yourself, go back and read the original scripture.

I feel like provoking you a little. All the disciples of the sacred masters were baptized by their gurus. It was a kind of unwritten rule. Why was it that Jesus let John the Baptist perform baptisms if he wasn't his guru? And why did Jesus speak about Elisha in one of his seven sermons on the mount?

Think about it for a while. I just want to point you in the right direction. Jesus and John the Baptist, disciple and master; Elisha and Elijah . . . Go through the scripture, and stop taking everything people tell you as the Word of God.

The universe is totally fair. It is so just in fact that it allows you to live out an entire lifetime believing in injustice, if that is your desire.

Competition does not exist

Before you start calling me names here, ask yourself sincerely what would happen if you stopped thinking about others as competitors.

'Everyone knows that in nature, the strongest always win out over the weakest.' At least, that's the popular belief.

If you believe this, you must be looking at a different nature from the one I am looking at because what I see is a natural world where everything is interrelated and all the species work together in close cooperation. At times, the strongest become the weakest and vice versa. I don't see any competition at all.

Behind every so-called competitor hides an ally. You need to use the Albert muscle to see it. If someone wants to copy you, instead of slamming the door in his face and going off to war, take a look at what new strengths this player can bring to you and forge a strategic alliance.

It might not always be possible, but this is the initial tack you should take.

> Competition is destructive. Once you eliminate fear and rely on universal justice to even things out, the competitive instinct quickly dies. If a competitor uses your ideas to make money, so much the better for you. The pendulum will swing your way. It always does.

I would even go so far as to suggest you pay your competitors to copy you! Use other humans like the cells of the human body use one another symbiotically.

In a certain way, we form a social community strangely like the cells of the body. What would happen if your left hand began to compete with the right for your brain's attention? Things would become terribly mixed up.

With these kinds of ideas, people regularly accuse me of being disconnected from the news and from reality. They're right. I don't live in their reality. I prefer my own. Thanks all the same.

And if you really want to know, I prefer smoking the newspaper to reading it.

Enemy number 4: opinions

We're having fun now, aren't we? I apologize for the headache this book might be giving you, but it's necessary pain. Hold on, there are only two more enemies we have to confront.

The next one is quick to be unmasked: opinions.

We live in a relative universe where all points of view are valid. When you cut to the chase, having an opinion means trying to impose your point of view on others.

The only ones who feel obliged to look for support from others when debating or defending their positions are those who are uncertain about what they believe.

> The only ones who need to obtain the support of others in order to compensate for the weaknesses of their points of view are those who are not themselves convinced of their beliefs.

Whatever happens to you is your own fault—yours and yours alone. As long as you try to blame what happens to you on others, you'll never get anywhere in life.

When you put that responsibility elsewhere than on your own shoulders, it just means you are putting not only your power into the hands of others but your freedom itself.

Another experiment to try: during the next three days, count the number of times that you try to defend an opinion. You'll be troubled by the results.

Tell yourself that every time you have these debates, you uselessly waste your energy and demonstrate publicly that you aren't convinced of your own beliefs.

Couple problems

Most endless discussion takes place right in the home, you remember, where part-ners make part-ially-thought-out promises.

➤ Dependence

Since the rate of divorce is so high, it is obvious that couples fail to apply the basic rules of the laws of success.

For example, as long as one of the partners needs the other, there is the risk of problems. If you need your partner, it means that you need him or her to do something to make you happy.

You have expectations. That's the problem.

When these expectations are not met, you are disappointed, even shocked. But if you have no expectations, you will never experience disappointment.

Difficult? Perhaps. But not at all impossible.

> You can only love someone completely when you don't need them any more. That is what unconditional love means. When there are no conditions attached, you have no expectations.

Not needing your partner does not at all imply that you have to have a job outside the home. It just means that if one member of the couple remains at home by choice, he or she must have his or her own regular income taken from the revenue of the other partner.

It's a decision you have to arrive at through negotiation.

> Avoid joint bank accounts!
>
> Avoid joint bank accounts!
>
> Avoid joint bank accounts!

The two biggest sources of conflict within a couple relationship are money and sex. The question of money can be solved by ensuring the autonomy and liberty of each partner once the responsibilities of common life have been shared. As far as sex goes . . .

➢ Managing your sexual energy

Just as with questions of money, the couple needs to have a well-established sexual policy.

Each partner should write down what he or she likes or dislikes sexually and should consult appropriate specialized books to develop sexual techniques. The agreed-upon hours for sexual relations should be chosen in advance and the choice of position debated at the Sunday family dinner, in public.

Ha, gotcha!

Were you really taking me seriously? I was just trying to see if you were following me like a robot or if your mind was still functioning.

Sex is the most powerful energy that exists in the universe. And its flow has to be managed just as we manage the generation of electricity.

> Dear, sir, your wife or girlfriend won't suddenly turn into a Victoria's Secret model if you don't play James Bond, enticing her regularly with new adventures and surprises.
>
> Madam, your husband or boyfriend will always be in a bad mood if the unrelieved pressure in his testicles is so great it inflates the veins in his arms.
>
> You don't need a course in sexual prowess to understand this!

Of course, sex is a fundamental part of life. But there is much, much more to it. (I can see I've got your full attention now. In fact, I've got you by the . . .)

Welcome to the universe of sexual transmutation.

Love flows directly from the transformation of sexual energy into a higher-level frequency. But you still have to begin by striking the match! And the perfect fire starter is sex.

A wise man named Bourbon Busset once said, 'Loving is not staring into each other's eyes; it's staring together in the same direction.'

How right he was. But of course, it's not always easy to look in the same direction as your partner when you're trying out an exotic position from the Kama Sutra.

Enemy number 5: routine

Close your eyes—well, almost—and try to visualize the following scene as you read.

Imagine yourself and your beloved on a fabulous fifty-foot yacht anchored just off a magnificent tropical island. The sea is turquoise, there isn't a cloud in the blue sky, and there is no sound but the waves under the torrid sun. You're in paradise.

You spend the night in ecstasy in the arms of your goddess or your Prince Charming. The next day, the sun rises again, strong and warm in the azure firmament. The weather is as calm as it was yesterday; the sea calm, waveless. Nothing but peace and beauty surround you.

You have now been anchored in the same spot for seven days, tasting this divine world of sea, sun, and peace.

It has been three months now. The sky is still blue, the sun burning brightly, the sea placid.

Gee, whiz, do you think we could have some noise, a wave or two, some rain, *anything?*

Routine destroys lives. You eventually get tired of even the most wonderful scenarios, and paradise can become a drag. You need change, variety.

The problem is that you are spending so much time on protecting what you already have that you become a prisoner of your self-created routine.

Once you have reached your goal, rather than trying to ensure your security, you have to throw everything overboard and try a new road.

That's adventurous; that brings excitement back into your life. You'll never be able to see new worlds if you're not prepared to leave the comfortably familiar shoreline behind you.

> Once you understand that what counts is not your destination but the path you take to get there, you'll have taken a giant step on the road to success.

In your business, you will cease comparing new projects to lottery tickets. You'll constantly create new adventures for you and your family.

You won't have any more patience for the subway-to-work-and-back-to-the-mattress rat race. And that's the meaning of the universe, a gigantic playing field brimming with discoveries.

God gets bored too!

What would you do if you were all-powerful, all-seeing, and could be in all places at the same time? Let me tell you, you would give anything to impose limits on your powers for the simple joy of being able to distract yourself and create new adventures.

Each and every human being is born to draw on a blank canvas. As Deepak Chopra says, 'Put some spice in God's life!'

> If the high point of your week comes on Friday night when you collapse on the sofa and veg out in front of a film on your home cinema, you have an awfully boring life!

Am I wrong? So much the better if I am. But you won't have an adventurous life plunked down in front of a TV movie. Movies aren't bad in themselves, but when they become the most important stimulus in your life, something is seriously wrong.

➤ Hurray, I've got a problem!

Have you ever tried to climb up a smooth wall?

Why don't you try it right now? Go ahead, I've got the time. I'll watch.

Can't do it, can you? Well, obviously, to scale that wall, you need something to grip. And those gripping points are the 'problems' of the wall.

> In short, you need to confront problems in order to grow. The bigger the problems, the more you'll grow with ease.

When I go to a company to talk about growth, I always want to know the five most important problems they have. Inevitably, when we look at these problems with the Albert muscle, we find that they always camouflage the most powerful levers for the company's growth.

For example, neurolinguistic programming (NLP) is the current rage. Okay, let's follow the buzz. Get up. Let's program a metabolic reaction in your body by associating it with a series of words.

Try this powerful tool whenever you face a problem. You'll see, it's totally miraculous.

It will allow you to develop your Albert muscle and to have the reflex to say to yourself 'What benefit can I get from this difficult situation?' or 'What can I teach myself or tell myself by going through this trying event?'

Are you ready? Let's go then.

Stand up and shout with your arm raised and your fingers making the V for victory, 'I'm in deep shit!'

I kid you not. Louder now.

Your car just got a flat tire. Shout it out: 'Yes, I'm in deep shit!'

The bag full of fragile groceries just fell apart in the supermarket parking lot. 'Yes, I'm in deep shit!'

Your computer crashes, and you realize you forgot to save the presentation text for tomorrow's sales meeting. 'Yes, I'm in deep shit!'

Feels good, doesn't it?

And you know what? It works!

Now you know why I suggested you read this section of the book in a quiet corner. I'd have liked to see if you dared jump up in the subway or at a coffee shop and shout, 'Yes, I'm in deep shit!'

The Allies of Success

Our enemies are numerous on the road to success. But you won't travel all alone. If you arm yourself with the four necessary states of mind (test every hypothesis, use your intuition, keep a mental age of four, and slip on your mental Teflon), you will be prepared to meet up with the allies who will help you out in your search for success.

The first ally: curiosity

Have you ever met a child who didn't ask you endless, sometimes embarrassing questions the whole day long?

The problem is that as the years go by, we are taught to ask fewer and fewer questions. We are told not to stick our noses into other people's businesses and to raise our hands before asking for something. This has the effect of destroying our natural reflex of enquiry.

If you want a life full of adventure, you'll have to re-inject this quality into your day-to-day existence. You're just not curious enough. So if your grandmother told you that curiosity killed the cat, forget her advice; love her, but ignore her old wives' tales.

> Let the word *why* escape your lips at least ten times a day, and each time, spend a while looking for the answer to your question.

It isn't enough to say that you are interested in a whole lot of things. You have to do research and experiment. Reading, watching, and reasoning are not at all sufficient. Remember: I hear, I forget; I see, I remember; I do, I understand.

Here's another test: did you go look in the Bible to see why I claimed that Jesus was the reincarnation of Elisha? No? Well then, you're really not curious enough.

Daddy, daddy, daddy

Each new day, my children teach me more and more about the art of curiosity, and if I let myself be drawn into their world of discovery instead of dismissing them, I always learn something useful and passionately interesting.

Timmy (he's five) recently asked me why adults appeared to enjoy doing so many things children aren't allowed to do, like smoking, swearing, drinking alcohol, and touching each other.

As I looked for an answer, I quickly concluded that there was no intelligent explanation that could justify these decisions. In my home, our kids are thus free to smoke and drink. But you know what? They don't like it! They quickly found alcohol and cigarettes to be boring and unpleasant. So they neither smoke nor drink. But they're free to do either one if they so choose.

Their curiosity has been satisfied, and both my wife and I are sure that they won't jump into cigarette and alcohol consumption with the vengeance displayed by people whose curiosity has been bottled up for ten years. When the cork pops after so many years of prohibition, imagine the pressure of all that pent-up desire. It's enough to drive people mad.

Curiosity has to be satisfied because, sooner or later, it will rise to the surface anyway. The longer it is suppressed, the more out of control it is when it surfaces. You should have seen the reaction of my daughter Charlie (she's nine) when she asked my wife to give her more details about sexuality and my wife told her to go and see her dad about it.

'Oh, no, Mom,' she replied. 'I don't want to know that much!'

That's the way it is. I keep no secrets from my kids.

Fish are the world champions of synchronized swimming

Have you ever closely observed a school of fish, watching the way it moves from one place to the next? Did you notice anything surprising? Come on, light up your curiosity a little. What's so odd about the way a school of fish moves?

It's that the fish all move together. But how do they do it? How do they all turn left or right (okay, port or starboard if you like) simultaneously? And, no, the leader doesn't make a little noise to tell his followers what to do next. There's no secret code either and no delay loop or beam of energy invisible to humans.

But they still move back and forth in unison. Don't you find that bizarre?

Now, if I've awakened your curiosity, you mustn't leave it frustrated. You have to find an answer to this strange but highly significant phenomenon. I feel like abandoning you now to your own devices to find out for yourself, but no, this time I'll be kind!

If there is no apparent signal that orchestrates this simultaneous movement, there must be something going on at another level. Could it be possible, for instance, that the fish all share a common brain? Yes, absolutely!

The studies of Dr Rupert Sheldrake—in particular, those about the 100th chimp (this is one you'll have to look up for yourself)—show that all the beings of a given species are linked by a phenomenon called the morphogenetic field.

In other words, all the fish are linked by the same very-high-frequency channel and communicate unconsciously by morphogenetic impulse. And if this is the case for fish, it is also the case for humans. The implications of this phenomenon are absolutely extraordinary.

If we are all, men and women alike, connected to the same collective brain, it would explain why certain scientific discoveries occur simultaneously in many countries. It would also explain why a three-year-old child can be totally comfortable with the ninety-five buttons on the DVD player, while we adults still have trouble finding the on–off switch!

Gosh, the possibilities are endless. I hope you fell right off your chair with this revelation. Seriously, just imagine what you could accomplish if you succeeded in consciously tuning in to the collective human brain.

Imagine the options life would extend to you if you could access the cumulative knowledge of the human race at will! Do you even have the slightest inkling of what you could accomplish with an ally like that on your side?

Do you seriously believe that the great spiritual masters, the gurus of the world of finance, and the great artists obtained knowledge, success, and inspiration at random, just by chance?

You think they practised meditation strictly for their public image?

Try it, and see what happens.

Snakes and doctors

Here's another why to consider: why is the symbol for medicine a mace surrounded by two snakes with a pair of wings at the top, a symbol also known as a caduceus?

I doubt that many doctors have taken the trouble to understand their own symbol because if they did, the pharmaceutical industry would become ill.

And what about you? Have you ever asked yourself this question?

Here's a hint: try sexual transmutation. (Ah! I see the sparkle return to your eyes.) This is the second time I have used this expression, but I didn't invent it. That honour goes to Napoleon Hill, a brilliant researcher who studied success from 1908 to 1928 by interviewing the 500 most successful entrepreneurs of his time and made reference to sexual transmutation as one of the best-kept secrets of the leaders of the world.

You'll find a few more details (but no more than that; for the hands-on experience, you have to attend workshops) in the section on the amplifiers of the laws of the Tao of business. For now, let me just point out how much your curiosity is stuck in low gear.

For most of the peoples of the world, the serpent is a symbol of sexual energy. Take the serpent in the Garden of Eden, for example. Or if you visit the magnificent pyramids at Chichén Itzá in Mexico (careful, the steps are high), you will find an enormous serpent biting its own tail, surrounding some of the structures. You can also see similar images in the temples of India (some of them exclusively to what is termed the phallus of Siva) and in China, particularly during festivals that feature street dancing.

The serpent is uroboros, and it represents the sexual energy that completes a full cycle within the body without any waste.

The caduceus, a veritable miracle remedy—back then, doctors did not choose a symbol for no good reason—signifies the rise of sexual energy up through the spinal cord to give wings to the spirit.

What, a physicist can't also be poetic? But I'm not only poetic, I really employ sexual transmutation.

Television: yes or no?

Television is a remarkable technological exploit, a wonderful instrument for amusement. But when it is watched thirty-five hours a week, it becomes a plague on society.

And thirty-five hours of watching the boob tube is the North American weekly average. Do you consider yourself average?

How can you awaken your sense of curiosity and develop a life of adventure if you have your umbilical cord attached to the remote control? After all, the worlds of morphogenetic fields and sexual transmutation are far above the plane of soap operas!

The second ally: insecurity

Now that you have awakened your sense of curiosity, you are closer and closer to making the leap of faith. What leap am I talking about? The one where you don't have a parachute, of course!

If the need for security is the sworn enemy of success, insecurity is by contrast its powerful ally.

I hope by now you have done the exercise of writing down the five most wonderful moments of your life and convinced yourself that they all were the result of your jumping head first into danger.

Do it! Don't just read about it. My words are worthless by themselves. My point of view is worthless too. Nothing written in this book has any value. The only thing that counts is your own experience.

Don't be satisfied with intellectual curiosity. Life on earth demands practical experience. That is why we are here. You are here by your own choice and desire for experience.

City of Angels

There are three essential elements for success, independent of what your undertaking is.

1. You have to clearly define what it is that you want.

We'll go through an exercise further on to help you with this, but you have to understand that if you do not formulate precise demands, nothing will change. This is the scientific concept called inertia.

A large rock that is rolling will not change direction, nor will it speed up or slow down unless some external force is applied to it.

You are like that rock; you have accumulated a momentum of beliefs and actions from the past.

The only way for you to give a new direction to your life is to apply some force to it.

That force is the choice of what you want, determined by clear and powerful thought.

Each thought becomes a form of pressure on the rock that is your life, helping to change its direction.

2. You have to believe that it's possible.

I regret to inform you that you are going to have to believe that what you want to succeed at is possible. That's right, I am talking about faith.

Before you reply that you have no religion, don't believe in God, and are an atheist, permit me to demonstrate to you that you do possess faith.

First of all, if you define yourself as an atheist, you are already a believer. You believe in the absence of God. The complete absence of God is equivalent to the absolute existence of God. In effect, in both cases, you believe in something universal, something whose absence or presence could have the name of God. So you see, you have faith after all. In the relative world, heat and cold are equivalent.

You cannot live without faith. Not yet convinced? Okay then.

Have you ever flown in a commercial airplane? Did you interview the pilot before take-off? Did you examine his credentials and make sure he actually had a pilot's licence? Did you check to be sure that he hadn't had a couple of beers over lunch? Did you look at the aircraft records to determine if all the proper maintenance had been performed on the plane?

You didn't? Good heavens, you really are a believer then! You put your life in the hands of total strangers and had absolute faith in them.

I always knew it. You do have faith.

So to return to my point, if you want to achieve anything, you'll first have to believe that it is possible.

3. Jump with no parachute.

Aha! Now we're at the heart of the matter. Now that you know what you want and you believe it is possible to achieve it, it's time to jump! You'll have to leap into the unknown without knowing how you're going to get there. Off you go, with no escape hatch, putting all your eggs in the same basket, without a parachute!

Since you like the movies, I'm going to suggest that you go see, or return to see, *City of Angels*, which is a remake of the magnificent German film *Wings of Desire*. In this movie, an angel wants to become human because he has fallen in love with a doctor. And as you will see, in order to realize his dream, he has to go through three stages: choosing, believing, and daring to jump.

> It's the same for you. You choose, you believe, and you jump. Taste all the excitement and adrenalin that come with insecurity. Try it—today.

The Ant and the Grasshopper

I'm sure that when you were in school, your teachers filled your head with Aesop's fables, those boring stories chock-full of lessons. Remember? Sure you do.

The Ant and the Grasshopper by BOA (Boring Old Aesop):

> The grasshopper, in song summer long did she strive, Then was foodless and hungry when cold winds arrived. Not a scrap of fly or of worm could she win, so she stopped at her neighbor's the ant, cried famine, and begging for food, a few grains until the spring said, 'I'll pay you 'fore August, I swear that's the thing.' But the ant makes no loans; that's

no character fault. 'What did you do last summer, when all
was aswelter?' 'Night and day I sang freely to all, gals and
fellers.' 'Sang did you? Had a ball then? I don't care a whit!
Now dance 'stead of dinner, you insect dimwit.'

All right, enough foolishness. But welcome to the world of my own fables.

The Ant and the Grasshopper by Pierre the Physicist:

> The ant, from toiling her entire life through,
> Found herself ruined when retirement came to.
> Not a smidgen of energy was left from her strife
> To fully enjoy the last years of her life.
>
> She knocked on the door of the grasshopper, her neighbour,
> To beg some ideas for fun as a favour.
>
> 'I'm bored,' she said, 'and I'll offer to pay you
> From all of my savings, grasshopper, what say you?'
>
> The grasshopper, no egoist, not her best trait, was unkind,
> Saying, 'What did you do except work yourself blind?'
> 'Day and night through, I laboured. I toiled hard, you see.'
> 'You toiled? Now it's time to ache regretfully.'

And long live insecurity!

The third ally: active passion

I'm about to ask you the most powerful question I have come across in more than twenty years.

If you dare to use this question without restriction, your life will take off, and you will receive all the glory you deserve.

You have to find the reason why you chose to appear on earth. You have to find your role in life!

Your role in the corpus infinitum

Let's use an analogy.

Imagine that all humans form a single body in the image of the human body. We are the individual cells of the infinite body, or corpus infinitum.

What do we call a cell that is in the wrong place in the human body? That's right, a cancer!

If you do not fully play your role on earth, you become a veritable cancer in the body made up of all human beings. And what do we do with a cancer-causing cell? Try every means to destroy it.

And that's how you'll end up if you don't define your role as quickly as possible.

> If everything is going badly in your life, if your finances, your marriage, your work, your health, and your social life are not to your taste, working on the symptoms is useless. Go to the root cause; you're not in the right place!

Find your role as quickly as you can and abandon everything else immediately. Stop hiding behind clichés like 'Yes, but I have responsibilities' and flee your present role.

Don't wait to win the lottery, saying, 'When I have enough money, I can do what I want.' It will never happen.

All the gold in the world

Here's the question you have to ask yourself.

But don't suppose you're going to find the answer all at once (so much the better if you do). Others, myself included, have spent as much as six months of their lives trying to find the answer.

Drum roll, please . . . What would you do if you possessed all the money in the world? What would you do if you could make money appear by simply snapping your fingers? What would you do once you owned twelve houses, went on fourteen exotic trips, and bought twenty-eight luxury cars?

> Figure out what you would do if you possessed all the wealth in the world. Then do it, and you'll have all the wealth in the world.

Money comes as a consequence of finding out what your role is on earth and playing it.

In other words, money won't come to you in this life until you understand that the more you play your true role, the more you contribute to the success of the whole corpus infinitum. In effect, the more you contribute to the health of the body composed of all humanity, the more this body will send you 'oxygenated blood'.

Money is like a blood transfusion. A cell of the body that plays its role efficiently receives pints of well-oxygenated, fresh blood every day.

For growth to occur, blood has to circulate. Are you familiar with any types of cells that congregate in a little blood pocket just in case they might be short at some later date? That's just what an RRSP is, or a pension plan.

The more you play your true role, the more powerfully the pendulum will swing back towards you. It's by playing your true role that you maximize your contribution to the universe. It follows that by playing your true role, you will reap the most rewards from the tree of life.

Stop counting, stop planning, stop trying to protect yourself.

Play your role over and over again. Play your role, and ask for a lot out of life.

The permanent orgasm

Take money out of the equation. Money is never a good guide. It's only a tool. Stop making it a destination.

Don't tell me, 'Pierre, if I had all the money in the world, I'd make investments.' What are you talking about? Make investments? Haven't you been listening to what I've been saying? You can make money appear. Why in the world would you want to get revenue from investments?

And don't tell me, 'Pierre, I've worked so long and so hard, if I had all the money in the world, I'd do absolutely nothing!'

What are you saying? If you did nothing more, you'd die of boredom. Retirement—that's just the beginning of the end. Of course, I'm talking about retirement from your true role in life, not retirement from a suffocating job you wouldn't work at for a second if you did have all the money in the world.

So retire immediately from that kind of job, and start playing your true role right now.

It isn't a job you're looking for. It's the adventure of your life!

But how do you know if you've really found your true role in life?

> Finding your role in life is like having an orgasm. If you have to ask if you've really made it, you're not there!

3

Action!

Go, Go, Go!

Your basic firepower is now in place. You have the right mindset, you can recognize your enemies, and you have identified your allies.

It's time to get going.

In this section of the book, I am going to give you the other munitions you need to allow you to build your dream life.

Most importantly, don't think too much about the concepts I'll present. Concepts in themselves aren't worth anything. You have to take action! Take action, and don't be afraid to make mistakes.

> Even the best baseball players strike out seven times out of ten.
>
> But they come to bat ten times out of ten!

Let's go! Put down this book, and telephone someone right now. Go on, do it. Place a call to whomever you want to set in motion the realization of one of your dreams.

I'll go over there and haul you right out of your easy chair if I have to. After all, I've found my role in life: kicking your behind!

The Tao: Seeking Equilibrium

A life crowned with success requires balance.

The problem is, for most people, equilibrium means conservatism. This kind of equilibrium unfortunately doesn't rhyme with success.

Finding balance doesn't mean seeking a boring life either. Think about the teeter-totter, you know, the long board in playgrounds where kids sit at either end and try to rock back and forth. There are lots of ways to attain equilibrium in this game.

You could, for example, put two children of identical weight each twelve inches from the central pivot. That would do it.

But it would be an awfully boring kind of equilibrium.

Kids naturally place themselves at the ends and rock back and forth until they find their own balance. That way, it's more fun.

Looking for balance is great. But for God's sake, look for it at the extremes.

> People who lead the best lives are well-balanced extremists.

'And the others?' you may ask. In life, there are the doers, the onlookers, and the ones who ask themselves what the heck is going on!

The three axes

The word *Tao* comes to us from Asia, and it means 'balance' or 'equilibrium'.

The Tao of business is the search for this balance in all the businesses in your life.

To help the brain and the intellect grasp this rather unusual concept, it would be useful to create some categories. They don't really exist, of course. They are just markers we'll set up to help us understand better.

Intuition doesn't need these markers, but the brain does. As long as you haven't tossed your brain in the trash (metaphorically, of course), we'll need these markers to make progress. For example, in nature, there is no such thing as separate states of solid, liquid, or gaseous matter. Nature has a continuous scale of frequencies, vibrations that determine these states. It is we who have created these states in order to better understand the natural phenomenon.

In the same way, we differentiate intellectually between the material, intellectual, and spiritual worlds. But in absolute reality, there exists no difference between them.

The material world is spiritual, the intellectual world is material, and the spiritual is also material and intellectual. There is really only one single immense consciousness.

Even physicists who study the infinitely small have concluded from their studies in atomic physics laboratories that the very act of observing a particle begets it.

As soon as we look, the particle appears as if by magic. If we stop looking—shazam!—it disappears. Fascinating, isn't it?

> We can conclude that the observer, the act of observing, and the observed object all display a simultaneous activity. Each one instantaneously gives birth to the other two.

The observer: that's the real you, your spiritual side.

The observation takes place using your intellect.

And the objects observed are represented by the material world.

If you really grasp the meaning of this conclusion, which was arrived at in the past by the spiritual masters and confirmed by even some of the most sceptical of physicists, like Einstein, you'll see that everything really occurs at the level of your thoughts.

The thinker, the act of thinking, and the thoughts themselves are three faces of one and the same reality. But you are most assuredly not just your thoughts. In fact, you can practise observing yourself think. The French philosopher-scientist René Descartes once wrote: 'I think, therefore I am.' Kind of a strange way to put it, if you ask me. What he should have written was 'I am, therefore I am able to think.'

Inasmuch as we are not just our thoughts, we can exist without thinking. In fact, we do it all the time—at night, in the deepest phase of sleep.

If we consider dreams, we can conclude that we are not just our bodies. During the deepest stage of sleep, when we are dreamless, we can also affirm that we are not our thoughts. All that we can know is that we slept well. So we did exist even in the absence of our thoughts.

Moreover, there is a kind of space between two thoughts, a pause, a void.

That space is the real you, the creative you, the 'god' you. (Take a deep breath. This is a giant step we're taking here.)

Our objective is thus to bring you to the point of being able to use your thoughts in order to balance all the facets of your life and allow you to find the Tao of business.

How to Choose Your Desires

Now is the time to choose what you want. After all, you're on vacation here. Go on, jump in with both feet!

Finding your role in life by asking yourself the question 'What would I do with all the wealth in the world?' will lead you to the connecting thread of your existence. Later on, you can spice up the trip by making the realization of your wishes easier to attain.

Some schools of thought—Buddhism, for example—recommend that desire be suppressed and eliminated. That is a legitimate and efficient path towards attaining a state of 'happiness'. But I find it extremely trying. I'm not saying the way of Buddha is not a valid option, only that it's not the option I prefer.

There are other roads. I know many ways to climb the mountain. If you meet a so-called master who claims that his is the only way to find the road to paradise, turn around and run and never look back.

The true masters—and I've met some—will tell you there are many roads. They'll talk to you about their own choices and then tell you to try out others in order to find the one that suits you best.

Personally, I prefer the path of desires. From my own point of view, there is no better way of eliminating a desire than to completely satisfy it. Stopping up desire only strengthens it, and sooner or later, it will explode in your face.

Money doesn't guarantee happiness; you're absolutely right about that. But you will never be completely convinced of the truth of this adage if you don't live through a time when you have lots of money. Remember, if you don't experience something yourself, you never really know about it.

Wonderful homes, luxury cars, and trips around the world won't bring you happiness. But again, unless you have your hunger for them sated, you will never be profoundly convinced of this either.

To attain absolute happiness, you have to be deeply convinced that it is to be found elsewhere than in the world of duality. So you might as well go for it flat out and satisfy your desires as fast as you can.

My view is that the quickest way to find God is to take the way of your desires. And who can say that your desires don't come from him anyway or from you or, well, from you and God together?

Waves or particles

To bring you closer to being able to choose your desires and understand how important the mastery of your thoughts and your emotions is, let me describe to you some elements of modern physics.

By the way, if you hated physics at school, you probably had a boring or overly conceptual teacher because, believe me, physics is undisputedly one of the most beautiful of sciences.

Here's proof: Did you know that a particle behaves as matter and as a wave of energy at the same time? In other words, an electron is not only a little solid ball (well, actually not all that solid) but is also a wave, much like a radio wave—both things at the same time!

And because you are made up of particles that behave both like billiard balls and radio waves, you too are simultaneously matter and wave energy.

> In other words, you are sitting here reading this book and, at the same time, vibrating everywhere else. Try that one on for size!

The German physicist Heisenberg was a twentieth-century genius who discovered that it is impossible to know both the position and the speed of a particle. If we know where the particle is, we cannot know its speed. This celebrated discovery, the uncertainty principle, won Heisenberg a Nobel Prize in physics.

What this means for you and me is that all possibilities exist simultaneously. Pick whatever you like; it already exists in the universe of probabilities.

Everything is programmed in advance.

All lives take place simultaneously.

Just take your pick of them!

And you take your pick through your thoughts. Your thoughts work just like a television remote control. When you watch TV, all the programs are playing at the same time even though you only watch one at a time.

If you lose interest in a program, all you do is press a button on the remote, and—alakazam!—you're on another channel. You can do the same thing with your life. It's no more difficult and takes no more time than switching channels. All you have to do is press the button.

So as soon as events in your life no longer satisfy you, change channels by changing the focus of your thoughts. For example, as long as you keep your mind on your money problems, you're going to keep on watching the same old program.

If you want to eliminate debts from your life, first you have to free them from your mind. You have to mentally thank them for their services that have supported you for so long and tell them you don't need them any more. Tell them you're ready to move on.

You should think of your life as a gigantic video store.

You go in, rent a cassette, take it home, and enjoy watching it. All the other films are there in the store, waiting for you whenever you want them. It is as easy to watch any single one as another.

Each and every scenario exists.

There are even people who love to watch horror movies. To each his own!

Controlling your thoughts

Everything really takes place in your interior world.

I know you're used to thinking that the exterior world precedes the interior world. But it isn't true.

Whatever you choose to experience in your interior world must, out of necessity (it's a universal law), materialize in the exterior world. The stronger, more precise and static-free your thoughts are, the quicker their physical manifestation will be.

You can even literally materialize what you wish by the simple force of your thoughts, but this requires an enormous amount of energy and concentration.

Thoughts are waves

Albert Einstein's famous and universally accepted formula, $E = mc^2$, tells us that all matter is really concentrated energy. A thought is a wave of energy. It follows that if a wave is powerful enough, it will be transformed into matter. This is a law of physics.

That's why it's so important to observe yourself as you think.

The fact that most people have so many problems in their lives is not a chance event. All you have to do is look at the way they constantly ruminate, always negative: 'Everything is going wrong', 'I'm in debt', 'my kids don't listen to me', 'my boss is a sadist', and so on.

Still, I am not proposing that you just use the power of positive thinking. My point is, apply the accepted principles of quantum physics in your life. Energy waves become matter when they are strong enough (or repeated enough).

This rule works as much for positive thoughts as for negative ones. And even better, the results are cumulative!

> Each time you think about something, your brain emits a wave of energy. This wave is added on to all the other waves you have ever generated and to the waves emitted by everyone else. When the sum of the waves is sufficient, there is enough energy for your wish to become reality.

Jesus said, 'Ask that ye shall receive.' The way you ask is through repeated thoughts. By thinking so much about how you have to work hard in life, you create an environment in which, quite naturally, you work hard. So don't complain about it. You got what you asked for!

Using your spinal antenna

There are eight miles of electrical wiring in your spinal cord.

You probably already know that when an electrical current goes through a wire, a magnetic field is instantaneously created around the wire and has a circular motion perpendicular to the direction of the current.

Electric motors also work this way. Even more interesting is the fact that when the magnetic field meets another electric wire, it induces a current in this wire too without the two wires needing to touch.

In the same way, each time you think of something, you create an electrical current in your nervous system. The current creates a magnetic field, which creates in turn an electric flux in the nervous systems of others by induction. Can you understand now why humour is so contagious?

Let's take it a step further. The more energy you have, the more powerful the magnetic fields you generate and the stronger the reception of your signal by others. Charismatic people unconsciously utilize this scientific law. Which explains an awful lot, doesn't it?

If you pick up the telephone to call someone only to discover that person is already on the line, having called you at the same moment, do you really think it is a random event? Not at all. You simply tuned in first to that person's magnetic wave.

Your spinal cord is a veritable receiving and transmitting antenna by which you send and receive waves or thoughts. There are seven nodes, often called chakras or wheels, where the concentration of nerve endings is more dense.

Many popular books talk about chakras, but hardly any discuss them scientifically. In a nutshell, each of these nerve centres acts literally like a cell phone. Each is programmed to receive selected frequencies of vibration.

Without entering into the mechanical complexity, let me just say that the lowest node receives the frequencies of self-protection and security. The seven centres are situated at the level of the coccyx and the genital organs, a little above the belly button (which is the centre of chi or energy), at the solar plexus, at the heart, at the throat, between the eyebrows (the third eye), and at the top of the cranium.

Since the nodes (wheels or chakras) are intimately linked to the spinal cord, that extraordinary network of the human body's electric wires, they constitute the most efficient mechanisms for controlling the body's antenna. If they are properly developed, they will allow a greater and greater direct contact with the collective brain described earlier.

The star of dreams

Now that you've grasped the scientific principle, it's time to use it.

There are two things to do.

First, choose your thought waves according to your desires.

Then, amplify these waves by increasing your energy level and minimizing any interference.

Simple, isn't it?

In order to choose your desires, I'd like to propose a method called the star of dreams.

Take a sheet of paper and draw a pentagram (a five-pointed star).

Since we are looking for the Tao, or equilibrium, we will break down the choice of objectives into five categories in order to cover all the possibilities open to us.

Above the top point of the star, write 'spirituality'.

At the point on the upper right, write 'people and life'.

At the lower right-hand point, write 'money, things, and leisure'.

At the lower left-hand point of the star, write 'personal growth'.

Finally, complete the star by writing at the upper left-hand point 'projects'.

That's it.

Now, take five other sheets of paper and write one category at the top of each sheet.

Well now, use a chronometer, a wristwatch, or a wall clock. This is the only time you'll be allowed to use them in this book.

You are going to time yourself as you do the exercise.

Start with the sheet entitled 'money, things, and leisure'.

You have three minutes in which to write down everything you want to obtain in your life that falls into this category (e.g. cars, trips, homes, collectibles, jewellery, earnings, planes, stereos—everything you can think of that is related to money, property, and leisure).

There is no limit in value to what you write. Everything is allowed. All options coexist simultaneously. (Remember the video store.)

And please feel free to dream in full colour. Or do you still have a black-and-white TV?

On your mark, get set, go!

* * *

That's fine.

Now take the second sheet, the one headed 'personal growth'.

Same instructions. You have three minutes to write down everything, even your wildest dreams, related to personal development (e.g. Spanish classes, piano lessons, magic, gardening, sexual transmutation, archery, becoming physically stronger and more flexible). Put it all down.

Pick up your pencil. Remember, there are no limits. Begin!

* * *

Super.

The third category is projects.

This category is for work-related projects, projects linked to your true role on earth, not your ridiculous and boring daytime job (e.g. start a company, found a charity, write a book, produce a music CD, build a house, open a school—whatever you like).

Take a deep breath and get going! You've got three minutes.

* * *

The fourth category is people and life.

Here, you are going to list all your goals relating to other living beings (e.g. have or adopt a child, choose a pet, take care of Grandma, join big brothers, get married).

Here we go, three more minutes!

* * *

The last category is spirituality.

This one is probably the most difficult, but it is as important as the others if you want to attain equilibrium and success. Here are some examples: meet a master, find the road to God, read the Bhagavadgita, practise meditation, and so on.

The last three minutes of thinking! Go.

* * *

You've already accomplished a lot. Isn't it great to let yourself dream in full colour?

Lasers or light bulbs

Right. Now you've got a list of dreams in your hands (and I really hope they are *big* dreams). Perfect.

How big is *big*? Big enough to excite you and frighten you.

> If your dreams don't give you the shivers, they're just not *big* enough!

Now you have to make some choices. However, before you get to it, you'll have to learn how to master the interminable flow of thoughts emanating from your brain that cause you to continuously lose energy.

Let's say you see someone with blue hair standing on the sidewalk. Suddenly, you find yourself thinking about an appointment with your hairdresser, then your sister-in-law whose hair turned green when she went swimming in a pool where the water was overchlorinated, and that turns into your youngest child's swimming class on Thursday that conflicts with your tennis lesson—oh, and your racket needs to be fixed, and . . . and . . .

Enough!

You start your days with seventy-eight things to do. You're constantly interrupted by phone calls and emails. You charge off in all directions at the same time. And you still wonder why everything takes so much time to get done?

Time to change gears. It's time to stop being a light bulb and start being a laser.

A light bulb sends its energy in all directions, and because of that, its rays can't even burn a hole in a piece of cardboard. A laser using the same quantity of energy can burn through metal sheeting because its energy is concentrated on a single wavelength. Each wave or vibration in the universe oscillates at a particular frequency and can be represented by an S-shaped curve of a particular length. The shorter the curve, the higher the frequency of vibration.

Here's an analogy. If you look at the strings of a piano, you'll see that the highest notes are produced by the shortest strings. A higher note means the string vibrates faster.

It's the same for light. A light bulb emits a large number of waves of luminosity of varying lengths all at the same time. Because the waves are distinct, some have an effect that is opposite to others and can weaken or cancel their power. The resulting effect is a modest amount of energy radiating in all directions.

The laser works in an entirely different way. Thanks to a series of complex lenses, the laser isolates a single type of light wave and amplifies it enormously in a single direction, hence the amazing power of the laser.

> Becoming a laser instead of remaining a light bulb signifies becoming truly obsessed.

When you become obsessed with something to the point of being unable to think about anything else, your brain becomes laserlike, and your thoughts can receive maximum energy. They can generate a magnetic field of great amplitude, and as a result, your desires can materialize a lot quicker.

If you want to accomplish something of value, you have to learn to shut down all the access points and reduce the losses of mental energy.

Take the writing of this book. I shut myself off from the world and wrote for five straight days—no phone calls, no emails, totally focused on this project.

If I had been at my office, I wouldn't have been able to put together two words without being interrupted. Why don't you do the following experiment? Try not speaking a word on Mondays for a whole month. Not one single word from sunup to sundown.

Since you won't be speaking, you won't be tempted to answer the phone. People will quickly figure out that you don't want to be disturbed on Mondays and will stop calling. In fact, I'm willing to bet that you'll get your entire week's work done in a single day. That's the power of strong focus; it gives you an amazing amount of energy.

Better yet, if you want to kick it up a notch, eat nothing on those days. Just drink water.

You'll feel more energetic than you ever did before. Don't ask why; it doesn't matter. Just do it!

Here's another one: get up in the morning with only one question to solve during the day.

Say to yourself, 'Today I want to solve only this one thing,' and all through the day, follow the path of coincidences (a concept I'll return to later on) related to this single preoccupation. Let everything else wait until tomorrow. And see how your life is changed dramatically when your brain has a laserlike focus!

Since we want your brain to have laserlike focus right away, you'd better choose which dream you want to come true first. If you think about what we have been saying, you can't have laserlike focus if you try to focus on ten dreams all at once.

Personally, after having tried a lot of different options—three dreams per category for a total of fifteen, five dreams in a single category, and so forth—I concluded that I was a lot more efficient when I only chose one dream at a time.

You'll have to find out what works best for you, keeping in mind the principle of the laser.

Questions or affirmations

Before you go ahead and read this how-to section, you're going to need to choose a single desire—just one.

Be sure that this desire is well defined and precise. For example, it is not enough to want to buy a house. I want to know how much land it has to sit on, what colours you want the walls to be, what kind of tiles you want in the bathroom—you know, everything!

If your wish is out of focus, you'll generate only vague waves and won't obtain the results you seek. So do your homework. Once you have a well-defined wish, you have a choice between two approaches: questions or affirmations.

The first method consists of asking questions of the universe and remaining conscious of the present moment to obtain its responses.

> These answers will always come from signs and undeniable coincidences.

The heart of the matter is, there are no coincidences. The events that you see as odd are there to wake you up, pull you out of your torpor.

If you dream about an old friend you haven't seen for a decade and he crosses your path the next day, cancel all your appointments, forget your schedule, and spend the whole day with him. He is the vehicle of the answers to your question.

But you don't believe me, do you? I couldn't care less; just give it a try!

The questions method consists of writing a precise question and watching for an answer to arrive. A question might be 'What is the best brand of piano to buy for me and the family?'

> Use the questions method if you aren't completely certain of the choice you need to make.
>
> However, if you know exactly what you want, use the affirmations method.

The affirmations method comes from the following principle: 'If you believe you have already received what you asked for in prayer, you will receive it.' Live as if your desires have already come true.

Go ahead, have fun with it, play the clown, fool around! Go into the living room and exclaim, 'Darling, I just love the magnificent way the new Steinway piano sets off the furniture, don't you?'

Behave as if the situation or the object is already there right before your eyes.

Now perhaps you understand better why this recommendation (Jesus said the same thing, by the way) is efficient. When you behave as if you already possess the object of your desires, you emit a stronger and sustained wave, and it all comes true.

Jesus wasn't just a preacher. He was preaching quantum physics.

How to Go about It and How to Measure Success

Let's finish up this section with a few additional bits of advice.

You already have a lot on your plate, and you can't really spend your whole life reading books. So let's sum up the global approach of *Ask and You Shall Receive* in a few words.

You are a very lucky individual. You are the chosen sperm cell, the one that won an extraordinary trip to this earthly paradise.

Everything in your life is the result of what you ask for and of your beliefs. Do what is required to use the beliefs that are useful.

Everyone is always right from their own point of view. Stop wasting your energy arguing with others. Keep your dreams to yourself.

Develop the four states of mind that are the prerequisites for attaining success by putting into practice one state of mind each week of the month: test, intuition, the mental age of four, and mental Teflon.

Challenge the enemies of success and learn to recognize your weaknesses.

Develop the three allies of success: curiosity, insecurity, and active passion.

As far as active passion goes, find your true role in life as quickly as you can and go for it—without a parachute.

Choose your wishes for each of the five categories of the star of dreams.

Train your brain to function like a laser. Only pay attention to a limited number of wishes and tasks at one time.

Use the questions method or the affirmations method to know how your wish will come true, paying attention to coincidences and special signs, keeping your mind solidly in the present moment.

That's the road we have travelled so far.

We can sum this up with the statement 'Ask and you shall receive'. Still, you were the one who decided to read through close to 150 pages to get to this one-liner!

Of course, building your faith does require a little work sometimes. Here are a few more suggestions before we ramp up to turbo mode.

Keep quiet!

You have nothing to gain and a lot to lose by sharing your dreams with others.

Since every thought that you have acts like a wave, the last thing you need is for someone else to emit a counterwave that cancels out the effect of yours.

If you want a house, don't discuss it with someone else in case they sow the seeds of doubt in your mind by saying things like 'Well, you know, a house is an awful lot of work and a pain if you want to travel. You'll have to hire someone to cut the grass, ask the neighbours to keep an eye out for burglars, stop the papers. I'm telling you, it's more trouble than it's worth.'

If you let even the smallest suspicion of doubt enter your mind, your wave is destroyed. Forget the house, wrap up the dream, it's gone!

> Keep your wishes to yourself.

The 3D mirror of your life

Learn to observe and interpret everything you see. Now that you know that the answers and the road to take will be revealed by out-of-the-ordinary events, stay alert. Stay in the present; stay conscious.

Learn to recognize too that everything your eyes show you is the mirror of your thoughts.

If your partner complains all the time about your family finances, you should ask yourself honestly if you don't share the same concerns. Stumble through the dark cave of your emotions to see if you too suffer from financial insecurity.

Tell yourself that if you had no problem with money, your external universe would simply not bring it up. Everything—absolutely everything—that your senses tell you is a reflection of your own beliefs, your own thoughts, and your own fears.

If you look at things from that perspective, you will be able to progress very quickly by relying on the recurring events of your life to better understand the road you have travelled and the distance left to go.

André's Porsche

A good friend of mine had long dreamed of buying a Porsche. For more than twenty years, André tried to suppress this dream and put it out of his consciousness since rationally he knew the purchase was extravagant and he didn't really believe that he deserved it.

But despite André's efforts, the desire for the Porsche kept resurfacing. It was a real obsession. Still not convinced he could afford the car (the classic excuse), he asked his wife what she thought. A true mirror of his own thoughts, she was quite naturally categorically opposed to this 'ridiculous indulgence'.

What a vicious circle! Every time I saw my friend, I encouraged him to make up his mind once and for all and to take the plunge, promising him that not only would the money come by itself once he himself had decided that he deserved the Porsche and that nothing in the world was going to stop him from having it but that his wife would also stop haranguing him about his 'foolishness'.

Eventually, the cork popped. André went to the dealership and bought himself a Porsche. When he showed it off to me two days later, his eyes sparkled like those of a child. It was really great to see!

One short month later, he told me that people were not treating him the same way as before, that he found he could easily get twice the price for his consulting contracts and that, miracle of miracles, his wife's attitude to the car had totally changed. She had suddenly developed a passion for going shopping in the Porsche!

The demons are inside you. The people around you are only mirrors. From this point of view, your family members are extremely precious to you, but they can also become extremely cruel.

In short, the closer your family members are to you, the more they will throw back in your face your own fears and your own qualms. Before criticizing them or fleeing from them, look within yourself and do some housekeeping.

Paradise on earth is a truly extraordinary place to be.

4

The Laws of the Tao of Business

A Mathematical Universe

What you have learned so far is enough to allow you to enjoy a fascinating experience in our earthly paradise.

That said, in order to be sure that I've convinced your rational brain, let me suggest to you the underlying functioning of the universe. Obviously, this explanation is based on my own understanding, experiments, and research.

The precision and the mathematics of the universe are truly impressive. Science reveals to us daily that our intellectual comprehension of the mechanisms of nature is almost non-existent. Just imagine: we live among millions and millions of planets and galaxies!

The immensity of the universe leads me to believe that the adventure is never-ending and that I will be able to grow towards even greater challenges once I have exhausted the experiences possible in this paradise on earth.

Moreover, in all the religions I have studied, I always find the same principle even though it is formulated in a variety of ways: one day or another, you have to be prepared to leave this paradise and go on to other things. But to what exactly? That's not easy to say. The answer depends on your concept of tourism!

For example, we could imagine a universe where duality has been replaced by *triality*, like a coin that can fall heads, tails, or on the rim; a universe without gravity; or one we see through our mouths.

Oh, I know this is a little far-fetched, but if the universe is infinite as some claim (and to my way of seeing things, this is a constructive and very exciting belief), why couldn't there exist other universes completely different from ours? Once we have finished trimming our own hedges, we might like to try something different and visit another universe.

I don't have a lot of details about these other 'islands'. Still, I do know that there exist detailed ways of leaving this one. I'm not here to tell you when to go. I am simply stating that there are escape hatches specially reserved for people who at some point will have experimented to the full the available options offered in this paradise.

Until that day comes, we have a lot of work to do, if only to understand the laws that govern our own universe. Everything I have been able to identify in my own research, both scientific and spiritual, can be summed up in seven great laws that I'm going to present now in shorthand version.

The objective of this book is not to explain each of these laws in detail, but to give your brain enough food for thought to inspire it to ask in order to receive—and to inspire you to take full advantage of your vacation here!

The law of action and reaction

It's the mother of all laws, the heart of the principle of perfect justice. The law of action and reaction is Newton's third law, and it teaches us that for every action, there is an equal and opposite reaction.

Get up and push against a wall. Go ahead, push. Do you know why the wall doesn't move? It's because the wall pushes you back with the same force, generating equilibrium and immobility.

Stop pushing now. How much did the wall advance towards you? It didn't? Well, you have stopped pushing, but why has the wall stopped pushing too? As far as I know, you have no mental power over that piece of drywall or concrete or wood, so it should have gone on pushing and moving in your direction, right? But it didn't!

Read this carefully: the simple fact of your choosing to push causes a simultaneous reaction in the wall. You push; it pushes. You stop; it stops.

Let's put it another way. The simple fact that you control one half of an equation means you really control all of it. The consequences of this are numerous and important. The most obvious is that you don't have to worry about finding answers.

> The most effective people don't waste time looking for answers. They spend time looking for questions.

In short, the simple fact of asking a question automatically generates a response. It's a law, the law of action and reaction. So don't break your back seeking answers any more; find the questions instead!

The universe hates disequilibrium

Our little wall experiment also shows us that the universe will always seek to maintain equilibrium. In physics, we learn that equilibrium tends to be situated where the energy required is the least.

Lazy son of a gun, the universe, isn't it? It respects the principle of the least effort.

Now, all creatures in nature follow this rule too—well, except, of course, the ones who are supposed to be the most intelligent, meaning the humans, the ones who prefer to work themselves crazy!

If you really want to create something, create disequilibrium in the universe. By generating a thought wave and launching it into the universe, you will have created disequilibrium.

Here's an example. You want to start a new company. Using the principles of this book, you go off in search of a detailed vision for this enterprise of yours. You define the solutions you will offer your clients, find office or plant space, determine how many employees you will require, figure out the size of the market and how many clients you will want, identify the best potential distributors of your product, etc. You now have a well-defined vision.

Great! Using this vision, you now send a new wave into the universe.

This wave takes the form of a desire. The more you think about it, the more you reinforce this wave broadcast by your spinal antenna. What you are doing is this: by maintaining that wave, you are creating a disequilibrium or disturbance in the fabric of the universe.

And the universe hates this—it doesn't like it at all!—just like you can't stand it when your neighbour plays heavy-metal music at ear-splitting volume in the middle of the night.

The universe has to respond. It has to shut you up. So either it gives you what you want (so you'll stop sending the wave) or you will destroy your own wave with destructive thoughts like 'A business is a lot of work. And risk. And competition. And responsibility. And management . . .' Get the idea? These thoughts cancel out your initial vision. Balance is restored, at least from the point of view of the universal equilibrium.

So only two things can occur here: either you will destroy your own thought wave with your doubts and fears or the universe will find a way to shut you up by answering your request.

Cool, ain't it?

The law of analogies

'Everything that exists up there is just like what we have down here.'

One of the most exquisite challenges of modern science is to explain the strange similarities between the infinitely small and the infinitely large.

Have you ever noticed the way atoms, with their protons at the centre and their electrons orbiting around it, so strangely resemble what we see in space: galaxies with suns and black holes in the centre and planets travelling around them in orbit? No, of course, you haven't. You're too busy making a living to think about things like that!

The genius Albert Einstein lived out his final years trying to resolve this enigma by linking nuclear energy (the infinitely small) to gravitational energy (the infinitely large).

He never succeeded, but he was able to state this: 'I just want to know God's thoughts. Everything else is details.' Don't you think that this is fascinating, that one of the world's greatest physicists talked about the thoughts of God?

According to the law of analogies, whatever is true in one domain holds true in all others. That is the symbol of the first card of the Tarot, one finger pointing upwards and the other downwards.

It is also the significance of the six-pointed Star of David or Seal of Solomon, which is formed by a triangle pointing upwards and another pointing downwards.

> This law shows us that whatever holds true in our thoughts and our interior world must, out of necessity, become true in our exterior world.

The law of creation

This is the heart of the 'ask and you shall receive' principle. The law of creation confirms that we are all creators and that our thoughts are felt by the rest of the universe.

Everything we have learned in this book about the creation of your life takes place through the application of the law of creation.

To show you to what degree matter has no veritable reality, let's make a miracle. But just before we do it, let me point out that the chair on which you are sitting does not really exist. It's true, I'm telling you! I haven't been smoking the newspaper this morning!

There is no chair under your behind right now.

The so-called chair is in fact made up of countless molecules, themselves made up of atoms, which are composed of electrons, neutrons, and protons. Are you with me so far? Right.

Hold on a sec. Okay, let's go on. A hazelnut compared to the size of the earth is about like an atom compared to a billiard ball.

Now, let's take that atom and blow it up to the size of a baseball stadium. The core of the atom would be about the size of a grain of sand inside the stadium. Looked at another way, the billiard ball is completely empty. If we looked at your chair under an electron microscope, it would look like a gigantic empty hole.

Are you ready for the miracle? Okay, lift your fist high in the air and slam it down on a table or against the wall. Go on, here, I'll help you. *Bam!* Did your fist go through the table? No? Great! You just made a miracle happen!

> The miracle is that we are able to create the illusion of touching something that in reality is completely empty!

Your mind is so powerful, it is capable of maintaining the illusion of your five senses out of nothing at all. You're quite something, you know.

The law of vibration and movement

When we look through the microscope, it's fascinating to see that the particles we think of as static are in fact moving all the time. Everything moves. The real truth is that not only does everything move but everything moves according to all the possible probabilities.

Our universe is one gigantic theatre containing multiple realities. Not only does everything move, but everything that moves vibrates at a favourable frequency.

This is the resonance principle. To better follow me in this short lesson in physics, take a guitar and pluck the G string. It starts to vibrate at its natural frequency and makes a sound.

But here's the extraordinary thing: if you place a second guitar right in front of the first, the G string of that guitar will start to hum all by itself without you touching it. It will be 'excited' at its natural frequency by the waves emitted by the first guitar and join the dance all by itself!

Try it. You'll see that it is a very convincing experiment!

According to the law of analogies, you and I also possess elements that bring us into resonance with others who absorb all our energy. That's why you trip out on some musicians (they resonate with you), while others make you run screaming from the room.

This is also why you sometimes have the impression that you know everything about a person you have only just met, while at other times, you feel incapable of liking someone who is a complete stranger.

When you keep your consciousness in the present, you are better able to choose the food, music, and colours that energize you and stay away from those that de-energize you.

The marvellous Hindu science of life, called Ayurveda, describes the individual types and frequencies in great detail. Feng shui, another very popular application of the law of vibration and movement, is a derivative of Ayurveda.

The law of the conservation of energy

Nothing is ever destroyed, and nothing is created. I'm sure you've already heard of this law; perhaps you've even used it. But do you really understand it?

Nothing is created. We do not create a thing. All we do is move energy around. Better yet, we don't really move energy around; what we move around is consciousness!

You are, before anything else, a big pile of consciousness.

If you want to augment your power, you have to limit your consciousness losses. You have to stop scattering your attention, radiating your energy in all directions.

Worries, stress, rage, envy, and even too-frequent ejaculation will empty out your consciousness. In the same way, the kind of food you eat will grow or shrink your level of consciousness. It holds true also for the kind of music you listen to. I can't guarantee what will happen to your consciousness level if you listen to the Smash Crashing Killer Potato Skins all the time.

But, hey, I'm not making a value judgement about your taste in music. Remember, no opinions! I make no pretension that listening to Hindu mantras or Gregorian chant is better than listening to heavy metal. It's just different.

Nor am I saying that being a vegetarian is better than being a meat eater. It's just completely different.

> I prefer Hindu mantras and vegetarian cuisine because they bring me a level of consciousness that suits me.

Here's the keyword: *different*. Do your own experiments, and then decide what is best for you.

I can nonetheless assure you that if you aspire to almost superhuman levels of energy, you will have to nourish your interior and exterior worlds with high-frequency elements.

In effect, if you want to lift your level of consciousness and understand why the great masters lost interest in material things, meat, and the ejaculatory orgasm, you'll have to get to that point yourself.

Is the life of a master that much better than yours? No, it's just different; that's the long and the short of it. It's all a question of choice.

When you have had enough of playing on earth, when you conclude that you've been weeding the same garden over and over, you will start to feel like you want to know something different. At that very moment, you will take on new points of view and emit higher-level frequencies.

Until then, apply yourself to fulfilling your craziest desires. Make them all come true so that when you leave, you'll be leaving on the right foot.

The law of evolution and the divine law

The sixth and seventh laws of the Tao of business concern choices for leaving this island of duality and our earthly paradise. Because of this, they will not be discussed in this book.

The Amplifiers of Success

The world of the Tao of business is made up of three parts:

1. The materialization of your dreams—this concept has been thoroughly discussed in the preceding pages.

2. The seven great laws that orchestrate the functioning of our universe—these we just finished explaining in brief.

3. A series of tools and practices that allow you to augment the power of these laws and accelerate the actualization of your desires—these we'll call the amplifiers of success.

There are enough tools and practices to fill many books. But I love interacting with the public. Once you have awakened your curiosity and have fully begun to taste the amazing power of the Tao of business, perhaps you will have the audacity to enrol in one of the workshops given by me or other quixotic researchers. (Check them out at www.pierremorency.com.)

Until then, here are samples of some good amplifiers.

Food

You are what you eat. Haven't you already been told that?

But I say it like this: you vibrate at the frequency of what you eat. You vibrate at the frequency of the colours you wear, the music you listen to, and the aromas you smell.

Don't fall into the jaws of the advertisers who try to push one kind of diet or another on you. Do your own experiments by trying a particular diet for a defined length of time and then analyzing its effects on you.

Suggesting the same diet for everybody is as ridiculous as forcing kids to go to school to follow all the same classes. A kidney cell can't possibly have the same development or the same needs as a cell from your thigh. Human beings are complementary in nature, not all the same.

Once more, I invite you to experiment with your own body. As for me, I have discovered that milk, almonds, mangoes, red wine, tomatoes, peanut butter, and natural yogurt make the best combination for maximizing my own energy levels.

But you have to find what is ideal for you according to the results of your own tests. Frankly (and I don't want you to take this as a value judgement), I don't think that you will be able to go into a deep meditative trance after a heavy dinner of roast beef. But you should try if you want to. My own sense is that it would be like trying to listen to Mozart while your neighbour in the upstairs apartment has Marilyn Manson on full blast.

Breathing or the science of prana

I have the distinct pleasure of telling you that you don't have only one body.

You've got three.

So next time somebody asks you if you're fiddling with your body, you'll have to ask, 'Which one?'

Our three bodies are: the physical, the astral, and the causal.

The physical body is the seat of matter, the astral body the seat of thoughts and emotions, and the causal body belongs to the thinker.

When you breathe, you don't only enrich your blood with oxygen. You also absorb prana, the equivalent of oxygen for the astral body. From Sanskrit origins, the word *prana* is the basis of an exceptional science that is called the pranayama, or mastery of the breath, in India.

It is precisely this prana that nourishes your consciousness.

I'll skip the details and just tell you that your causal body has 72,000 channels for the circulation of prana called *nadis*.

'What can this change in my life?' you ask. Well, look, when prana is abundant and circulates freely throughout the astral body, your thought waves have exceptional power. I think you can guess the rest.

Good breathing means that oxygen is carried all the way to the abdomen. Most adults don't really breathe. They take in short breaths, and they survive, but they don't breathe. You want to solve your weight problem? Nothing could be easier. Relearn to breathe.

Digestion is a process of combustion. Have you ever tried to light a fire without the presence of oxygen? So how do you expect to efficiently 'burn' your food if you don't send enough oxygen into your system after you eat?

Breathe actively for three minutes after each meal, taking deep breaths and sending the air all the way down to your abdomen. You'll be surprised by the results and quickly toss out your powdered diets and diet bars.

Believe me, the science of pranayama is truly a wonder. It teaches us a host of practices for stimulating the circulation of prana in the nadis so as to permit cleansing the system of all the blockages accumulated over the years.

But it is definitely not a science for the faint of heart or for conservative souls.

Reprogramming beliefs

Now we're on familiar ground.

The best way to reprogram a belief is to construct a sentence and repeat it over and over, such as 'I will permit myself to be rich' or 'I'm feeling better and better every day'.

The application of scientific principles to the good old concept of positive thinking should allow you to grasp the power of a phrase repeated mentally over a given period of time without stopping.

If the beliefs (or the 'ham stories') that fill your head right now come from your education, your family, and your entourage, your new beliefs have to come from voluntary reprogramming.

The fastest way to destroy one belief and replace it with another is still the repetition of a thought, which can take the form of a short phrase or phrases. For example, if you believe it is impossible for you to double your revenue this year, you might use the following sentences: 'This year, I will double my earnings. The ideas about how to accomplish it will come to me easily. I'll recognize them instantly.'

By repeating these phrases regularly, you will eventually reprogram yourself. Since you now know the physical principles that are behind this phenomenon, you can also say that by emitting this new thought wave, the universe will enter a state of disequilibrium and will answer your new demand by following the law of action and reaction.

It's not exactly rocket science!

If you want more examples, I leave you in the capable hands of Joseph Murphy and *The Power of Your Subconscious Mind*. This book was my introduction to personal growth, and even if I was only nine when my grandfather read it to me, it remains for me one of the great classics on the subject of reprogramming beliefs.

Controlling frequencies

This amplifier is an expanded version of the explanation I gave in the section on nutrition. Since everything vibrates, you must study the impact of everything that surrounds you on your energy level. What use is it to make a whole program of desires and dreams if you haven't got an ounce of energy left to give to them because all the juice has been pumped out of you by an exterior factor?

Let me give you an example: How do you feel after watching TV for three consecutive hours? Wiped out? This is understandable because the frequency of the waves emitted by the apparatus tends to destroy your energy reserves.

Music is an excellent way to begin to master and control the frequencies that occupy the space around you. To convince you that this is so, take two plants of the same kind (ideally, two cuttings from an original plant), and place them in two different but equally sunny spots in your home. Water them identically at the same time of day.

Now, play some Mozart to one plant for four hours a day, and give the other one four hours of heavy metal.

Try this experiment; you'll see that the results are surprising.

You can also experiment with colours. See how you feel after two hours in a room dominated by a red colour scheme compared to, say, a yellow one. I learned about that in 1994 on a trip to Las Vegas when I ate at the Luxor Hotel's Manhattan buffet. The restaurant, in operation from 1993 through 1996 before undergoing major renovations, was divided into five single-colour sections: red, yellow, green, blue, and black. And when I say single colour, that's just what I mean; everything in one section was in the colour assigned to it—the tables, walls, floors and ceilings, plates, glasses, staff, even the food!

We were seated in the red section. After ten minutes, the tension was so high between us that we decided to leave before we began throwing the dinnerware at each other!

Too bad they didn't reopen the place after the renovations. I learned there the real meaning of the sentence 'Never doubt the influence frequencies have on your life.'

Sexual transmutation

If there is one subject in my estimation that books should leave in peace, it is sexuality. At the same time, the masters describe sexual energy as the fundamental power that drives the universe. So this notion is central to my approach.

What makes me laugh is that every time I start to bring up the notion of sexual transmutation, people react by thinking, 'Right, here we go, he's going to talk about abstinence. He's going to tell me that if I aspire to a richer spiritual life, I'd better scratch sexuality out of my life.'

Not at all. The idea is not to prescribe abstinence; that would be ridiculous. Abstinence can be a very positive thing, true, but it must never be forced on you. It comes naturally when your system is ready for it and when your energy channels have been cleansed.

What happens when you keep pouring water into a glass? It overflows eventually. So what good does it do to impose abstinence on yourself and then lose all your energy in night-time erotic dreams?

As long as the nadis are not purified, sexual energy will have trouble climbing the stick. Think about Moses, who spent forty years in the desert trying to 'get the serpent to climb the stick'. You follow? No? Well, let me help you out a little.

Sexual energy fuels your entire system. If you want to create something, you need your energy reserves. This energy can be channelled along your spinal column to get your antenna up and running.

The day that you understand that the energy that makes everything work is, at its core, sexual, you'll never again view sexuality the same way. Sexual energy is marvellous!

I'm going to share with you a very simple technique to help 'the serpent climb' and allow you to taste something different from what I like to call the simple orgasm. Then I'll shut up about it.

So from now on, think about sexual relations as if it were a pressure cooker.

- Turn on the gas or the electric element. That's the sexual arousal phase.

- Don't remove the cover. You there—especially you, sir—you must absolutely learn to hold back. How? Use breathing. (Practise slowing down your respiration, and little by little, let your arousal climb up your spinal cord.) If you have to, pause regularly for a couple of minutes.

- Eventually, the 'steam' will find the little valve, like the hole at the top of the cooker. This little valve is something we all have at the bottom of the spinal cord. When energy begins to flow through it, prepare yourself for a real ride!

Modern physics has demonstrated that every particle has its opposite. An electron is the opposite of a positron, matter is the opposite of antimatter, etc. When a particle is combined with its opposite, matter is destroyed and replaced by an enormous amount of energy. Remember Einstein's equation, $E = mc^2$, where E represents energy and m mass. According to this equation, by combining opposite particles, we convert them into energy. If this is true for subatomic particles, it's true for you. And the sacred texts tell us that sexual energy can return to its source to combine with its opposite.

That is what the many ancient images and sculptures of gods and goddesses shown in sexual union tell us. The most famous of these is, without a doubt, the one in which the god Shiva sits in a meditative position, back straight, with his wife, the goddess Shakti, sitting on him face to face, her legs around his waist in full sexual intercourse. This is exactly the symbolism used to show transmuted divine sexual energy.

The most ancient writings (such as the Vedas) almost always present the divinity in the company of his feminine half to remind us that we can attain God by raising the level of our sexual energy. Why? Because this sexual energy situated at the base of the spinal antenna changes frequency at the moment of its ascension, changing from explosive animal energy to a transcendent and divine form.

My experiments and my research have brought me to conclude that true love (I sense here some women may resent me for this) is nothing more than sexual energy that has risen to the level of the fourth chakra, i.e. the heart. That's right. Sex and love in fact are one and the same! They're the same thing, but at different frequencies. Now, be careful. Tasting all these experiences requires discrimination. Quickies on the clothes dryer in the laundry room can be fun, but I swear they can't hold a candle to the vibration of the caduceus.

I'll stop now. Have I whetted your appetite? So much the better. Turn off the darn television and investigate a little with your partner.

Meditation

Meditation is a voluntary act in which we connect to the collective brain at the highest frequencies to try to taste different states of mind and to enter into contact with different frequencies from those of the whirlwind of our daily thoughts.

You can meditate on endless things, but the most interesting subjects of meditation are, in my view, the seven chakras and the divine images. Concentrating your thoughts on various positions of your spinal antenna, you can activate them and better grasp their usefulness.

And divine images? An image of God (pick the one you like) vibrates at an enormously higher speed than our normal thoughts. By concentrating your mind on one of these images, you can literally catapult your consciousness towards indescribable frequencies.

I'm afraid that quantum physics will be of no use to you here. Not my fault; faith begins where science ends. And yet, the most important principle of physics is completely applicable here. Experiment!

In the Bible, it is written that Jesus said, 'When you want to speak to God, be silent, go into your room, and listen.' In other words, enter into a meditative state and concentrate your thoughts on God. He'll do the rest.

True meditation, performed with an accomplished guide, is one of the most wonderful experiences I have ever had. It's my first priority when I get up in the morning.

The asanas or yoga positions

The true sense of the word *yoga* is 'union', union with the divine.

The positions, breathing exercises, and concentration are all aspects of yoga. These positions, called asanas, are much more than just exercises for developing flexibility.

Physical flexibility is, of course, an excellent benefit of yoga, but it is not its first objective.

The main goal of yoga is to concentrate your thoughts in order to facilitate the mastery of the body and the cleansing of the nadis of the astral body so as to favour a better circulation of energy. Each asana is meant to cleanse a specific part of the body both physically and astrally.

Some of the positions are almost magical. My favourite is standing on my head (literally upright but upside down). By reversing the flow of blood for a few minutes each day, you let your heart rest in a way it can't when you are prone. The heart works upside down for a bit, and this rest allows for a considerable improvement in its efficiency and helps it stay healthy.

There are many books on yoga. It is a methodical practice that can bring you considerable benefits. Once more, it is recommended that you practise this discipline under the supervision of a qualified teacher.

I hope this brief review of the amplifiers of success has awakened your curiosity. Now it's time to put yourself into success mode!

What about Happiness?

When I described our universe as a relative world where everything works through paired opposites, I was alluding to the pleasure-pain coupled opposite. I wrote that happiness would be the exception to the rule of duality.

Unfortunately, finding happiness on earth is about as probable as finding peace and quiet in a day-care centre. 'So', you ask me, 'why is life worth living?' This is my reply: 'For the pleasure of tasting everything that this relative world can allow us to experience.'

Why eat, dance, or even become parents when we know our children will eventually grow old, suffer, and die?

Because we love adventure. We live to learn, create, and play.

If not, we would fall into an infernal routine of wanting to have everything and know everything. Remember the experiment where we visualized life on a yacht for three straight months?

At the end of the day, everything, even life in paradise, becomes boring.

That's why we always have to create new adventures for ourselves.

Everything is a mystery, and it's a good thing it is

Why hurry to look for total understanding? Why should we want to read the last line of a book as soon as we have finished the first paragraph? Play the game instead, and follow the path of your desires.

Play the script, knowing that there are no real victims, no real problems, nothing more than a play and its actors. Does this idea shock you? Then maybe you are too attached to your own sense of self-importance.

I'll say it once more. We are all practically dead already. There is no reason to accelerate the process with all your worries and your fears. Follow the desires that appear spontaneously in the real you, and one day or another, the game will end. One fine day, you'll really feel like experiencing something different. When that day arrives, you will know it sincerely and without hesitation, and like others before you, you will put on your backpack and plunge into the depths of your consciousness to find your way off the island.

But there's no hurry. A whole eternity awaits you.

True happiness is forever

Everything that has a beginning and an end belongs to the relative world. Absolute happiness has neither beginning nor end. On earth, we're just out for a good time.

If you really think you are on this earth to find happiness, here is another challenge: stop having sex and alcohol for the next thirty days, and only eat bread, almonds, and fruits and only drink milk and water.

See if your days are as interesting as before.

See if you still feel like going out or developing new projects. See if the promotion you wanted is really as important as it seemed before. See if you still want a new car.

Try the test. I can guarantee that once the thirty days are over, you'll have no interest left in anything. You'll understand that the pleasure–pain pair presupposes sexual gratification, a varied diet, sleep, play, and security. If you cut yourself off from sexual pleasure, variety in your diet, and diversity in your play, paradise on earth loses its meaning.

Accept the fact that you want sexual gratification, toys, good meals, and adventure. And play the game. When the game is over, you will quite naturally pass on to the next phase.

Believe me, you won't do it with a heavy heart or a sense of loss. You'll do it with eyes wide open and with complete satisfaction.

Lucky or unlucky: the art of being non-judgemental

When we begin to seriously study the path to happiness, we are confronted with the need to be non-judgemental. We discover that we need to place ourselves above the good–evil couple and cut ourselves off from it.

Judging others gets us nowhere.

Make your choices, take a point of view that suits you, and go forward.

Let others waste their energy by being judgemental, argumentative, and opinionated.

Let me tell you a little story.

It concerns a man who is married and have children and who worked in government, in the tax collection department. One fine day, by mistake, his son received a $3,000 tax refund in the mail; it was just enough to cover his fees in the faculty of engineering at university.

His friends said, 'You're so lucky! What do you intend to do with the money?' The son had learned from his father that everything in life happens for a reason and that the concepts of luck and misfortune don't exist. Not knowing the money was sent in error, he replied, 'Well, I don't know if the money came by luck or through misfortune, but I'm going to use it to pay my tuition.'

The following month, police officers came to his father's office to arrest him for fraud on suspicion of having illegally caused money to be sent to his son.

Upon hearing the news, the son's friends went over to see him. 'Talk about bad luck! Your dad's in jail, and your family's reputation is in tatters. What will you do now that you haven't got the $3,000 any more and you have to take care of your family while your dad's being held?'

The son, calm as ever, replied, 'I already told you, I don't know if all this is the fault of luck or misfortune. I suppose it's something we just have to go through in order to grow. Every cloud has a silver lining, so I have to keep my mind open and not judge things.'

Two months later, the father was released from prison, and the government made an official apology for the dreadful mistake. In order to compensate for the trouble caused, the government promoted the father and gave the son free tuition at a university of his choice!

The son's friends returned once more. 'What incredible luck you have! You can choose whatever university you want. Tell us what saints you pray to so we can do the same!'

Now, tell me, was this boy lucky or unlucky? Neither. He simply received what he needed on each occasion.

Practise the art of not judging things. Tell yourself that whatever happens, it is always for the best.

You just have to ask yourself, 'Why is this happening to me now?' and try to understand the message.

Free will or destiny

Are we free or bound by fate? This is truly a fundamental question for us as we study happiness.

I'm not sure my answer will make you happy. We are both free and bound by fate. You are simultaneously free and a puppet.

Here's an analogy: Imagine yourself at the wheel of a Formula 1 race car, driving along at 150 miles per hour, and I suddenly tell you to make a left turn. Are you free to do it? Well, yes and no.

You aren't free to do it immediately because you have to slow down first. Once your speed is reduced, you can make the turn.

Did anybody oblige you to drive that fast? No, you used your free will to attain that speed. But once you took that decision, you put limits on your future free will. Do you follow?

> Every time you use your freedom, you bind yourself to your fate because you have created that fate yourself.

To be really free, you must no longer use that freedom. Meditate a little on this idea.

Bhakti and *jnana*

The roads that lead 'off the island' can be put into two large categories: the path of devotion (bhakti) and the path of knowledge (jnana).

In the first case, you suppress your ego and place yourself in a state of servitude until God (your real you) comes to you.

In the second case, you destroy your ego by infinitely expanding it and find your divine state.

The Catholic, Muslim, Hebrew, Buddhist, and Hindu religions all essentially follow the path of devotion.

One way or another, you will attain a divine state. The choice is, do you want to taste the honey or become the honey?

Here's an analogy to explain our relationship with the divine: Imagine a field with thousands of buckets brimming with water. It's midnight, and the moon is full.

From a hill above the plain, a child looks at the field and the water-filled buckets and, seeing the reflection of the moon in each bucket, says, 'There are so many moons on earth.'

In fact, there is only one moon and thousands of reflections of the moon just as there is only one god. You and I are each a reflection of that same divine source.

So this is your real goal on earth: play the relativity game and create, create, and create again so that at the end of the road, you will have become a better god.

Conclusion

Dear partner on this voyage, I want to thank you for having accompanied me on this short trip through the Tao of business.

You have seen that as a physicist, I can explain many things with ease, but I can also make them more complicated.

And I was only warming up! Whenever you like, we can go off into the world of quarks and neutrinos.

If you prefer, we can also discuss mantras, *nada* yoga, and the life of Krishna. Not a problem. I'm a fan of every religion and every experience.

If our only reason for existence was to eat, sleep, have sex, and defend ourselves from danger, we wouldn't be much in the end. Think of it. A lion's life would do as well or better. A lion eats what it wants, has everything it needs to defend itself from its natural enemies, has sex with twenty lionesses who do all the work for it, sleeps twenty hours a day, and get this, the lucky stiff can have up to fifty orgasms a day. Pig orgasms, on the other hand, are less frequent but can last up to half an hour each!

'So what are we doing in this human skin?' you might ask. There must be a reason for it.

And there is. We have the immense privilege of being able to consciously participate in the creation of new adventures and the tasting of other levels of consciousness. And we have the indescribable pleasure of being able to ask anything we want of the universe.

So what are you doing working eighty hours a week?

Why are you wasting your time watching four hours of television a day?

Why are you still reading this book?

Don't waste a single minute more.

Just ask and you shall receive!

Don't go where the road takes you.

Leave the road and break
your own trail.

Leave a trace of your passage on
this island paradise on earth!

Ask and You Shall Receive

Is it possible to combine a full spiritual life to a successful career and to family life? Not only is it possible but absolutely essential! Like always, the marketing and success physicist did his homework. Loyal to the scientific method, he travelled across India and studied various religions and spiritual masters to bring you back a complete and applicable spiritual path.

Ask and You Shall Receive is a retreat for professionals and company leaders who absolutely want to find how to use and apply the laws of success (true scientific laws) and concrete spiritual practices in their businesses and personal lives.

Meditation (no, not any kind will do!), specific yoga and breathing techniques for business people, knowledge on universal rhythms, the power of sexual transmutation (you've read correctly!), the mastery of coincidences, how to reduce your sleeping hours, and even the birth of a connection with God will be presented in this very unique retreat for entrepreneurs who just know that there's more than plain rational stuff out there.

Finally, someone with spirituality for the business world, backed up by scientific knowledge—real, tangible, and very useable knowledge.

If you are dedicated to finding a well-balanced yet sparkling life, you won't want to miss *Ask and You Shall Receive*—an amazing mystical experience!

Coming soon at 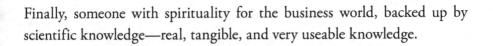www.pierremorency.com

For more information, call 514-761-0040 or 1-866-morency.

Printed in the United States
By Bookmasters